KIM DIEHL

Simple Whatnots IV

A MIDNIGHT SNACK OF SATISFYINGLY SCRAPPY QUILTS

C&T PUBLISHING
Another Maker Inspired!

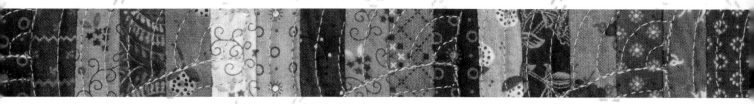

Text copyright © 2024 by Kim Diehl

Photography and artwork copyright © 2024 by C&T Publishing, Inc.

Publisher: Amy Barrett-Daffin

Creative Director: Gailen Runge

Senior Editor: Roxane Cerda

Editor: Karen Costello Soltys

Cover/Book Designer: April Mostek

Production Coordinator: Tim Manibusan

Illustrator: Missy Shepler of Shepler Studios

Quiltmaking Basics illustrations by Sandy Loi

Photography Coordinator: Rachel Ackley

Front cover and lifestyle photography by Adam Albright Photography, Inc.

Cover and lifestyle styling by Jennifer Keltner of Snappy Style

Subject and instructional Photography by C&T Publishing, Inc., unless otherwise noted

Published by C&T Publishing, Inc., P.O. Box 1456, Lafayette, CA 94549

Library of Congress Cataloging-in-Publication Data

Names: Diehl, Kim, 1959- author.

Title: Simple whatnots IV : a midnight snack of satisfyingly scrappy quilts / Kim Diehl.

Other titles: Simple whatnots 4

Description: Lafayette, CA : C&T Publishing, [2024] | Summary:

"Best-selling author Kim Diehl is back again with spectacular, small, and scrappy projects. Inside quilters will find 20 delightful quilts that feature traditionally pieced blocks, Kim's signature invisible machine appliqué, wool appliqué, and more. These scrappy charmers are perfect for any quilter"-- Provided by publisher.

Identifiers: LCCN 2024018137 | ISBN 9781644035252 (trade paperback) | ISBN9781644035269 (ebook)

Subjects: LCSH: Quilting--Patterns. | Patchwork--Patterns. | Patchworkquilts. | BISAC: CRAFTS & HOBBIES / Quilts & Quilting | CRAFTS & HOBBIES/ Sewing

Classification: LCC TT835 .D52536 2024 | DDC 746.46/041--dc23/eng/20240501

LC record available at https://lccn.loc.gov/2024018137

Printed in China

10 9 8 7 6 5 4 3 2

Contents

Introduction

For as long as I can remember, quilts have been part of my life. As a little girl, I slept under my grandma's hand-sewn quilts and loved counting the pieces, looking at the beautiful prints, and running my fingers over the stitches that held everything together. When I grew up and had a family of my own, on a whim, I set about teaching myself how to sew a quilt, and I fell in love with them all over again.

Since there are only so many beds in need of quilts, and there are so many designs just waiting to be made, I began stitching my quilts in smaller and smaller sizes, and "whatnots" were born! These little quilts can be tucked into the smallest niches, nestled onto tabletops, rolled into crocks or baskets, racked and stacked, or displayed on your walls.

In addition to being versatile, small whatnots can bring big opportunities. You can treat them as skill builders and dabble in new techniques, or even stretch yourself and tackle more advanced block designs, knowing that the finish line is in sight right from the very start. Best of all, unlike large quilts, with no long-term commitment needed you can be fickle and jump from project to project with a completely clear conscience. No judging happening here!

In this fourth installment of my Simple Whatnots series, I've included many of my personal favorite designs in the hopes of serving up a truly scrumptious midnight snack of mini quilts. And to further sweeten the "Diehl," of the nineteen quilts included in this collection, six projects are brand new and designed just for you.

Gather your favorite scraps and prints, rev up your sewing machine, and stitch to your heart's content!

~ Kim

County Fair

Is there such a thing as too many Churn Dash quilts? No way! This tried-and-true block has been loved by generations of quiltmakers for good reason—it's versatile, full of humble charm, and a snap to piece. Set these sweet blocks among simple hourglass units, or tweak the cream and dark positions slightly, and one basic block suddenly takes on two distinctly different looks.

MATERIALS

Yardage is based on a 42″ width of useable fabric after prewashing and removing selvages.

- 1 fat quarter (18″ × 21″) of black print for patchwork and binding
- 24 chubby sixteenths (9″ × 10½″) of assorted prints for patchwork
- 5 skinny eighths (4½″ × 21″) of assorted cream prints for patchwork
- ½ yard of fabric for backing
- 18″ × 31″ piece of batting

CUTTING

Cut all pieces across the width of the fabric in the order given unless otherwise noted. For the Churn Dash A and B blocks, cutting is provided for one individual block to enable you to easily plan your print and color choices; simply repeat the cutting to produce the needed number of patchwork sets.

From the black print, cut:
4 binding strips, 2½″ × 21″ (for my chubby binding method on page 126, reduce the strip width to 2″)
Reserve the remainder of the black print for the patchwork blocks.

Hourglass Blocks

From *each* of 10 of the assorted chubby sixteenths, cut:
1 square, 4¼″ × 4¼″ (combined total of 10); cut each square in half diagonally *twice* to yield 4 triangles (combined total of 40).
Keep the triangles organized into an Hourglass set; reserve the remainder of these assorted prints.

As your scraps permit after cutting all required pieces for this quilt, you may wish to cut a handful of additional squares and cut them into triangles for scrappier blocks.

From *each* of the 5 assorted cream prints, cut:
1 square, 4¼″ × 4¼″ (combined total of 5); cut each square in half diagonally *twice* to yield 4 triangles (combined total of 20).
Add the assorted cream triangles to the Hourglass set; reserve the remainder of the assorted cream prints for the Churn Dash blocks

Churn Dash A Blocks

From *all* assorted prints, including the remainder of the black and previously used prints, choose 4 prints per block. You'll need 8 sets of 4 prints. From each set, cut:
1 square, 1½″ × 1½″ (center square, from one print)
1 strip, 1″ × 7″ (side inner rectangles, from a second print)
1 strip, 1″ × 7″ (side outer rectangles, from a third print)
2 squares, 1⅞″ × 1⅞″; cut each square in half diagonally *once* to yield 2 triangles (total of 4; corner inner triangles, from the fourth print).
Keep the pieces organized into a Churn Dash A set.
Repeat to cut a total of 8 Churn Dash A sets.

Continued on page 10

Continued from page 9

Churn Dash B Blocks

From the scraps of *all* assorted prints, choose 4 prints per block. You'll need 3 sets of 4 prints. From each set, cut:

1 square, 1½" × 1½" (center square, from one print)

1 strip, 1" × 7" (side inner rectangles, from a second print)

1 strip, 1" × 7" (side outer rectangles, from a third print)

2 squares, 1⅞" × 1⅞"; cut each square in half diagonally *once* to yield 2 triangles (total of 4; corner inner triangles, from the fourth print).

Keep the pieces organized into a Churn Dash B set. Repeat to cut a total of 3 Churn Dash B sets.

From the remainder of the assorted cream prints, cut a *combined* total of:

6 squares, 1⅞" × 1⅞"; cut each square in half diagonally *once* to yield 2 triangles (combined total of 12). Choosing the prints randomly, add 4 cream triangles to each Churn Dash B set.

40 squares, 2" × 2". Keep these squares organized into a flying-geese set.

4 additional squares, 2" × 2"

From the remaining scraps of all assorted prints, cut a *combined* total of:

20 rectangles, 2" × 3½". Add these rectangles to the flying-geese set.

PIECING THE HOURGLASS BLOCKS

Sew all pieces with right sides together using a ¼" seam allowance unless otherwise noted. Press the seam allowances as indicated by the arrows or otherwise specified.

1. From the Hourglass Block set, randomly select two print triangles and two cream triangles. Lay out the triangles in two diagonal rows as shown, above right. Join the triangles in each row. Press. Join the rows. Press.

2. Repeat to piece 10 scrappy Hourglass blocks measuring 3½" square, including the seam allowances.

Please note that you'll have a handful of unused assorted print triangles; these have been included for added choices as you piece the patchwork.

Make 10 Hourglass blocks, 3½" × 3½"

PIECING THE CHURN DASH A BLOCKS

1. Select one Churn Dash A set. Join the two assorted print 1" × 7" strips along the long edges. Press. Crosscut the pieced strip at 1½" intervals to make four strip-set segments measuring 1½" square, including the seam allowances.

Make 1 strip set. Cut 4 segments, 1½" × 1½".

2. Choose the 1⅞" triangles cut from two assorted prints. Layer two triangles, one from each print, together. Join the pair along the long diagonal edges. Press. Trim away the dog-ear points. Repeat to piece four matching half-square-triangle units measuring 1½" square, including the seam allowances.

Make 4 half-square-triangle units, 1½" × 1½".

3. Lay out the four half-square-triangle units, the four strip-set segments, and the 1½" center square in three horizontal rows. Join the pieces in rows and then join the rows. Press. The pieced Churn Dash A block should measure 3½" square, including the seam allowances.

4. Repeat steps 1–4 to piece a total of eight Churn Dash A blocks.

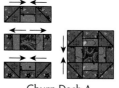

Churn Dash A
Make 8 blocks, 3½" × 3½".

County Fair

FINISHED QUILT SIZE: 12½″ × 24½″ ✦ **FINISHED BLOCK SIZE: 3″ × 3″**

Designed and pieced by Kim Diehl. Machine quilted by Connie Tabor.

PIECING THE CHURN DASH B BLOCKS

Using the Churn Dash B sets, repeat steps 1–4 of "Piecing the Churn Dash A Blocks" to piece a total of three Churn Dash B blocks that have cream triangle corners. The blocks should measure 3½" square, including the seam allowances.

Churn Dash B
Make 3 blocks, 3½" × 3½".

PIECING THE FLYING-GEESE UNITS

1. Use a pencil and an acrylic ruler to draw a diagonal sewing line from corner to corner on the wrong side of each of the 40 cream 2" squares.

2. Choose a 2" × 3½" print rectangle from the flying-geese set. Layer a prepared cream square onto one end of the rectangle. Stitch the pair along the drawn line. Fold the resulting inner triangle open. Press. Trim away the layers beneath the top triangle, leaving a ¼" seam allowance. In the same manner, add a mirror-image triangle to the remaining end of the rectangle. The pieced flying-geese unit should measure 2" × 3½", including the seam allowances.

3. Repeat steps 1 and 2 to piece a total of 20 flying-geese units.

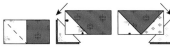

Make 20 flying-geese units, 2" × 3½".

PIECING THE QUILT TOP

1. Lay out two Churn Dash A blocks and one Hourglass block in alternating positions. Join the blocks. Press. Repeat to piece a total of four Churn Dash A rows measuring 3½" × 9½", including the seam allowances.

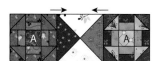

Make 4 Churn Dash A rows, 3½" × 9½".

2. Lay out two Hourglass blocks and one Churn Dash B block in alternating positions. Join the blocks. Press. Repeat to piece a total of three Hourglass rows measuring 3½" × 9½", including the seam allowances.

Make 4 Hourglass rows, 3½" × 9½".

3. Refer to the quilt center assembly diagram to lay out the Churn Dash rows and the Hourglass rows in alternating positions. Join the rows. Press. The pieced quilt enter should measure 9½" × 21½", including the seam allowances.

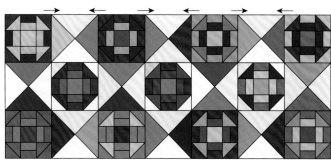

Quilt center, 9½" × 27½"

4. Join seven flying-geese units end to end. Press. Repeat to piece two long flying-geese border strips measuring 2" × 21½", including the seam allowances.

Make 2 long flying-geese border strips, 2" × 21½".

5. Join three flying-geese units end to end. Press. Join a cream 2″ square to each end of the pieced strip. Press. Repeat to piece a two short flying-geese border strips measuring 2″ × 12½″, including the seam allowances.

Make 2 short flying-geese border strips, 2″ × 12½″.

6. Join the long border strips to the right and left sides of the quilt center. Press. Join the short border strips to the remaining ends of the quilt top. Press. Use a rotary cutter and an acrylic ruler to trim away the outer cream triangle portion of each corner square, leaving a ¼″ seam allowance.

Completed quilt top, 12½″ × 24½″.

COMPLETING THE QUILT

Layer and baste the quilt top, batting, and backing. Quilt the layers. The featured quilt is machine quilted with an edge-to-edge chicken wire design. Join the black binding strips to make one length and use it to bind the quilt..

Token of My Affection

For as long as I can remember, scrappy quilts have been a part of my life. I grew up surrounded by my grandma's "blankies" pieced from the smallest bits of saved scraps, and quilts filled with tiny snippets of favorite prints still speak to me today. I encourage you to comb through your scraps, rescue the smallest pieces of cloth, and transform them into this twinkling mini.

MATERIALS

Cut all pieces across the width of the fabric in the order given unless otherwise noted.

- 1 fat quarter (18″ × 21″) of dark print for patchwork and binding (I chose navy)
- 27 bitty bricks (4½″ × 10½″) of assorted prints for patchwork
- 4 fat eighths (9″ × 21″) of assorted cream prints for patchwork
- ⅔ yard of fabric for backing
- 24″ × 24″ square of batting

CUTTING

Cut all pieces across the width of the fabric in the order given unless otherwise noted.

From the fat quarter of dark print, cut:
4 binding strips, 2½″ × 21″ (For my chubby binding method on page 126, reduce the strip width to 2″.)
Reserve the remainder of the dark print for the patchwork.

From the 27 bitty bricks and the remainder of the dark print, cut a *combined* total of 64 quarter-star patchwork sets, with each set consisting of:
1 square, 2″ × 2″; cut each square in half diagonally *once* to yield 2 triangles (combined total of 128)
1 matching-print square, 1½″ × 1½″

From *each* of the 4 cream prints, cut:
2 strips, 2″ × 21″; crosscut into 16 squares, 2″ × 2″ (combined total of 64). Cut each square in half diagonally *once* to yield 2 triangles (combined total of 128)
2 strips, 1½″ × 21″; crosscut into 16 squares, 1½″ × 1½″ (combined total of 64).

PIECING THE QUARTER-STAR UNITS

Sew all pieces with right sides together using a ¼″ seam allowance unless otherwise noted. Press the seam allowances as indicated by the arrows or otherwise specified.

1. Select one patchwork set (with the prints collectively referred to as "dark" from this point forward). Then, randomly select two cream triangles and one cream 1½″ square; these should not be matching.

2. Join a dark and a cream triangle along the long diagonal edges. Press. Use a rotary cutter and an acrylic ruler to trim the unit to 1½″ square, removing the dog-ear points in the same step. Repeat to piece a total of two half-square-triangle units.

Make 2 half-square-triangle units
from each patchwork set, 1½″ × 1½″.

3. Lay out the two half-square-triangle units, the matching dark print 1½″ square, and the cream 1½″ square in two horizontal rows as shown. Join the pieces in each row. Press. Join the rows. Press. The pieced quarter-star unit should measure 2½″ square, including the seam allowances.

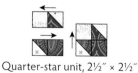

Quarter-star unit, 2½″ × 2½″

4. Repeat steps 1–3 to piece a total of 64 quarter-star units.

FINISHED QUILT SIZE: 16½″ × 16½″

Designed and pieced by Kim Diehl. Machine quilted by Connie Tabor.

PIECING THE CENTER-STAR UNIT

Lay out four quarter-star units in two horizontal rows. Join the units in each row. Press. Join the rows. Press. The pieced center-star unit should measure 4½" square, including the seam allowances.

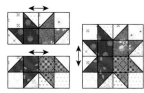

Center star unit, 4½" × 4½"

PIECING THE HALF-STAR UNITS

Join two quarter-star units in mirror-image positions as shown. Press. Repeat to piece a total of 12 half-star units measuring 2½" × 4½", including the seam allowances.

Make 12 half-star units, 2½" × 4½".

PIECING AND ADDING BORDER #1

1. Join a half-star unit to the right and left sides of the center-star unit. Press. The center-star unit with side border #1 units should measure 4½" × 8½", including the seam allowances.

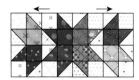

Center star with side border #1, 4½" × 8½"

2. Join a quarter-star unit to each end of two half-star units as shown to piece two top/bottom border #1 units measuring 2½" × 8½", including the seam allowances.

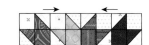

Make 2 top/bottom border #1 units, 2½" × 8½".

3. Sew the border units from step 2 to the top and bottom of the center-star unit, making sure the star points point away from the center star. Press the seam allowances toward the border units. The quilt top should measure 8½" square, including the seam allowances.

PIECING AND ADDING BORDER #2

1. Using two half-star units and four quarter-star units, repeat step 2 of "Piecing and Adding Border #1" at left to make two side border #2 units measuring 2½" × 8½", including the seam allowances.

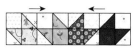

Make 2 side border #2 units, 2½" × 8½".

2. Join the border units to the right and left sides of the quilt center, with the star points pointing away from the quilt center. Press the seam allowances toward the new borders. The quilt top should measure 8½" × 12½", including the seam allowances.

3. Using two half-star units and eight quarter-star units, piece and press two top/bottom border #2 units measuring 2½" × 12½". Sew these border units to the top and bottom of the quilt center with the star points pointing away from the center. Press the seam allowances toward the border units.

Make 2 top/bottom border #2 units, 2½" × 12½".

PIECING AND ADDING BORDER #3

1. Using two half-star units and eight quarter-star units, repeat step 3 of "Piecing and Adding Border #2" above to piece and press two side border #3 units measuring 2½" × 12½", as shown.

Make 2 side border #3 units, 2½" × 12½".

2. Join the side border #3 units to the right and left sides of the quilt center with the star points pointing away from the quilt center. Press the seam allowances toward the border units. The quilt top should measure 12½″ × 16½″, including the seam allowances.

3. Using two half-star units and 12 quarter-star units, piece and press two top/bottom border #3 units measuring 2½″ × 16½″.

Make 2 top/bottom border #2 units, 2½″ × 18½″.

4. Referring to the assembly diagram, join the step 3 units to the top and bottom of the quilt center to complete the quilt top. Press.

Quilt assembly

COMPLETING THE QUILT

Layer and baste the quilt top, batting, and backing. Quilt the layers. The featured quilt is machine quilted with an edge-to-edge chicken wire design. Join the 2½″-wide dark strips to make one length and use it to bind the quilt.

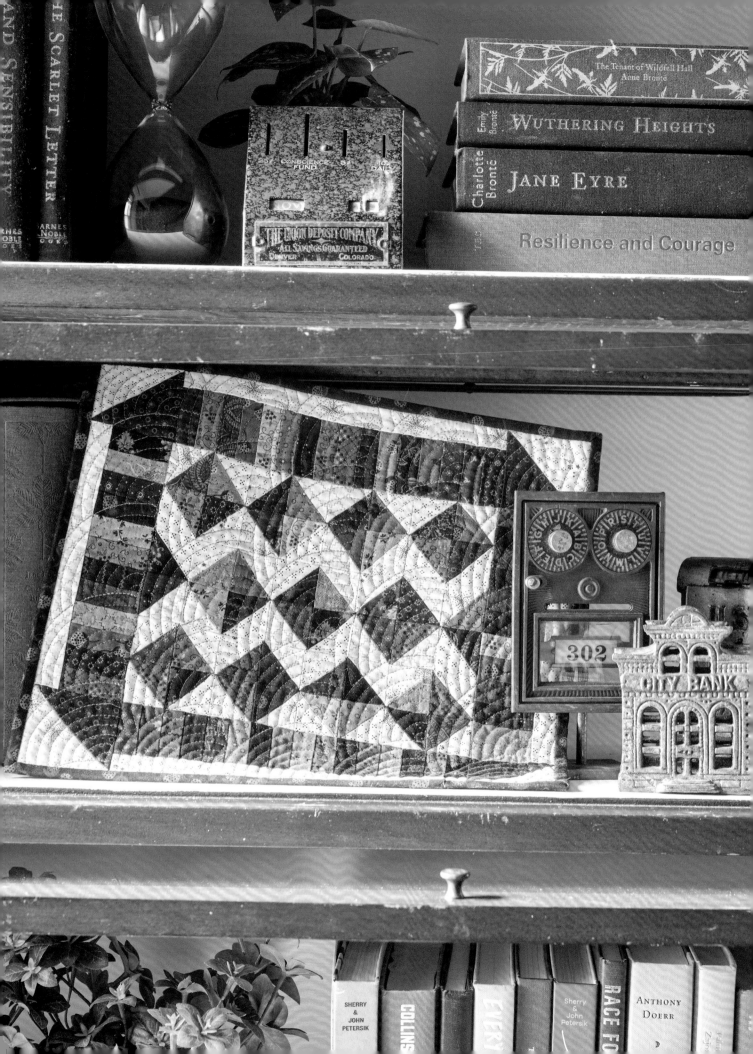

Safe Keeping

Take any traditional quilt block, make it tiny, and a little magic begins to happen. Patchwork honestly doesn't get much cuter than the scrappy "diamonds" sparkling in the 6″ × 8″ center of this mini quilt—until you surround them with a piano-key border inspired by the long-favored Churn Dash block. Proof positive that good things do come in small packages!

MATERIALS

Yardage is based on a 42″ width of useable fabric after prewashing and removing selvages.

- 26 charm squares (5″ × 5″) of assorted prints (referred to collectively as "darks") for patchwork
- 4 chubby sixteenths (9″ × 10½″) of assorted cream prints for patchwork
- 1 bitty brick (4½″ × 10½″) of navy print #1 for patchwork
- 1 fat quarter (18″ × 21″) of navy print #2 for patchwork and binding
- ½ yard of fabric for backing
- 16″ × 19″ piece of batting

CUTTING

Cut all pieces across the width of the fabric in the order given unless otherwise noted.

From *each* of the 26 dark prints, cut:

1 square, 2″ × 2″ (combined total of 26). Cut each
   square in half diagonally *once* to yield 2 triangles
   (combined total of 52)
2 rectangles, 1″ × 2″ (combined total of 52)
Keep the triangles organized into a dark triangle set.
Organize the rectangles into an dark rectangle set.

From *each* of the 4 cream prints, cut:

1 strip, 2″ × 10½″; crosscut into 5 squares, 2″ × 2″
   (combined total of 20); cut each square in half
   diagonally *once* to yield 2 triangles (combined total
   of 40).

1 strip, 3″ × 10½″; crosscut into:
   1 square, 3″ × 3″ (combined total of 4); cut each
   square in half diagonally *once* to yield 2 triangles
   (combined total of 8)
   1 square, 2″ × 2″ (combined total of 4, grand total
   of 24 with previously cut squares); cut each square
   in half diagonally *once* to yield 2 triangles (combined
   total of 8, grand total of 48 with previously cut
   triangles)
1 strip, 1″ × 10½″ (combined total of 4); trim 2 of the
      rectangles to 1″ × 8½″. Trim the remaining
      2 rectangles to 1″ × 6½″.
Keep the cream pieces organized by size.

From navy print #1, cut:

1 strip, 3″ × 10½″; crosscut into:
   2 squares, 3″ × 3″; cut each square in half diagonally
   once to yield 2 triangles (total of 4)
   1 square, 2″ × 2″; cut the square in half diagonally
   once to yield 2 triangles (add these to the dark
   triangles set for a combined total of 54 triangles)
1 strip, 1″ × 10½″; crosscut into 2 rectangles, 1″ × 2″
      (add these to the dark rectangle set for a combined
      total of 54 rectangles)

From navy print #2, cut:

3 binding strips, 2½″ × 21″ (for my chubby binding
      method on page 126, reduce the strip width to 2″)
1 strip, 2″ × 21″; from this strip, cut:
   1 square, 2″ × 2″; cut in half diagonally *once* to yield
   2 triangles (Add these to the dark triangle set for a
   combined grand total of 56 triangles.)
   2 rectangles, 1″ × 2″ (Add these to the dark rectangle
   set for a combined grand total of 56 rectangles.)

Successfully Stitching Small Patchwork

For mini projects that include small-scale pieces such as the narrow rectangles in this Safe Keeping border, accuracy is especially important to ensure the final pieced units come together beautifully. When stitching projects like this, there are two steps I consistently use to help me achieve great results.

First, *before* cutting, I give each print a misting of Best Press (a starch alternative) to firm up the body of the fabric and add stability, pressing each fabric one at a time with a hot iron as I build stacks of five or six prints for efficient cutting.

Second, I adjust the position of the needle in my sewing machine to produce a seam allowance that's a couple of threads *less* than a true ¼″. This slightly narrower seam allowance helps to compensate for the tiny bit of fabric that's lost to the fold of the seam when it's pressed open. If your sewing machine doesn't allow for the needle position to be adjusted, simply feed the patchwork under the presser foot with the fabric edges positioned a couple of threads away from the ¼″ guide. To ensure my adapted seam allowance is producing the desired results, I stitch a quick test piece by joining three rectangles, 1½″ x 3½″, side by side along the long edges, and then measure the width of the middle piece to ensure it is 1″ wide. If my results aren't spot on, I tweak my seam allowance until I'm satisfied with the result, and then continue stitching.

FINISHED QUILT SIZE: 10½″ × 12½″

Designed and pieced by Kim Diehl. Machine quilted by Connie Tabor.

PIECING THE PATCHWORK UNITS

*Sew all pieces with right sides together using a ¼"
seam allowance unless otherwise noted. Press the seam
allowances as indicated by the arrows or otherwise
specified.*

1. Using the dark print triangle set and the cream
2" triangle set, choosing prints randomly and join a
cream and a dark print triangle along the long diagonal
edges. Press. Use a rotary cutter and an acrylic ruler
to trim the unit to measure 1½" square, removing the
dog-ear points in the same step. Repeat to piece and
trim a total of 48 half-square-triangle units. You'll have
a handful of leftover dark triangles; these have been
included for added choices as you stitch the patchwork.

Make 48 half-square-triangle units, 1½" × 1½".

2. Join two half-square-triangle units with prints that
complement each other along the dark edges as shown.
Press. Repeat to make a total of 24 pieced rectangle
units measuring 1½" × 2½", including the seam
allowances.

Make 24 pieced triangle units, 1½" × 2½".

3. Join two pieced rectangle units to make a square-
in-a square unit measuring 2½" square, including seam
allowances. Press. Repeat to piece a total of 11 square-
in-a-square units. Reserve the two remaining pieced
rectangle units for later use.

Make 11 square-in-a-square units, 2½" × 2½".

PIECING THE QUILT CENTER

1. Join four pieced units end to end. Press. Repeat to
piece a total of two outer patchwork rows measuring
2½" × 8½", including the seam allowances.

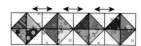

Make 2 outer batchwork rows, 2½" × 8½".

2. Join the three remaining square-in-a-square units
end to end. Sew one of the reserved pieced rectangle
units to each end of the row to make the center
patchwork row that measures 2½" × 8½", including the
seam allowances. Press.

Make 1 center patchwork row, 2½" × 8½".

3. Join one outer patchwork row from step 1 to
each long side of the center patchwork row. Press.
The pieced quilt center should measure 6½" × 8½",
including the seam allowances.

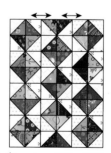

Quilt center, 6½" × 8½".eps

PIECING AND ADDING THE BORDER

1. From the dark print rectangle set, select 16 of the
1" × 2" rectangles randomly. Join the rectangles in
pairs, then join the pairs to make a pieced border unit
measuring 2" × 8½", including the seam allowances.
Press. Repeat to piece a total of two pieced border
units. Sew a cream 1" × 8½" strip to one long edge of
each pieced border unit. The borders should measure
2½" × 8½".

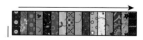

Make 2 pieced border units, 2½" × 8½".

2. Using two sets of 12 dark rectangles and two cream 1″ × 6½″ strips, repeat step 1 to piece two short border units measuring 2½″ × 6½″, including the seam allowances.

Make 2 pieced border units, 2½″ × 6½″.

3. Sew four different cream print 3″ triangles to the four navy #1 triangles along the long diagonal edges to make four half-square-triangle units. Trim the units to 2½″ square, including the seam allowances. Discard the remaining cream triangles.

Make 4 half-square-triangle units, 2½″ × 2½″.

4. Referring to the assembly diagram, join a long border unit from step 2 to each long side of the quilt center. Press. Join a navy and cream half-square-triangle unit to each end of the remaining two short border units as shown. Press. Join these pieced units to the top and bottom of the quilt center. Press.

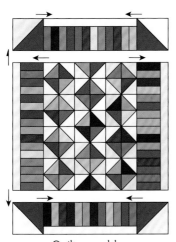

Quilt assembly

COMPLETING THE QUILT

Layer and baste the quilt top, batting, and backing. Quilt the layers. The featured quilt is machine quilted with a small-scale edge-to-edge Baptist Fan design. Join the navy print #2 binding strips to make one length and use it to bind the quilt.

Coffee Break

What began as a sewing experiment during a coffee break when I was goofing off (instead of tackling the projects on my to-do list) unexpectedly took on a life of its own. After starting with small rectangles and then stitching, layering, cutting, rearranging, and stitching again, I found myself with the most gloriously scrappy little blocks I'd ever sewn. A series of simple borders frames the patchwork beautifully and brings a wonderful sense of balance to this cheerful quilt.

MATERIALS

Yardage is based on a 42″ width of useable fabric after prewashing and removing selvages.

- Approximately ⅓ yard *total* of assorted-print scraps (enough to cut 48 rectangles, 1¼″ × 3½″) for blocks and border #1
- 1 fat eighth (9″ × 21″) of cream print for borders #1 and #3
- 1 fat quarter (18″ × 21″) of dusty aqua stripe or print for border #2 and binding
- 1 fat quarter of print for backing
- 18″ × 21″ piece of batting

CUTTING

Cut all pieces across the width of the fabric in the order given unless otherwise noted.

From the assorted-print scraps, cut a *combined* total of:

48 rectangles, 1¼″ × 3½″; organize these rectangles into a patchwork block set.

28 squares, 1½″ × 1½″; organize these squares into a border #1 set.

2 rectangles, 1½″ × 1¾″

2 rectangles, 1½″ × 2¼″

Add the 1¾″ and 2¼″ rectangles to the border #1 set.

From the cream print, cut:

2 strips, 1½″ × 21″; crosscut into 12 rectangles, 1½″ × 2½″

2 strips, ¾″ × 21″; crosscut into 2 strips, ¾″ × 13¼″

2 strips, ¾″ × 21″; crosscut into 2 strips, ¾″ × 12″

From the aqua print, cut:

2 strips, 1¼″ × 21″; crosscut into 2 strips, 1¼″ × 12¼″

2 strips, 1¼″ × 21″; crosscut into 2 strips, 1¼″ × 10½″

4 binding strips, 2½″ × 21″ (for my chubby binding method provided on page 126, reduce the strip width to 2″

PIECING THE PATCHWORK BLOCKS

Sew all pieces with right sides together using a ¼″ seam allowance unless otherwise noted. Press the seam allowances as indicated by the arrows or otherwise specified.

1. From the patchwork block set choose four assorted rectangles and sew them together side by side along the long edges. Press. Repeat to sew 12 pieced squares measuring 3½″ × 3½″.

Make 12 pieced square units, 3½″ × 3½″.

2. Choose two pieced squares. Lay one pieced square on your work surface with the rectangles positioned vertically. Layer the second pieced square onto the first pieced square, right sides together, and the rectangles positioned horizontally. Repeat with the remaining pieced square units, layering them into six pairs.

Layer pieced squares in 6 pairs.

3. Use a straight pin positioned diagonally in each corner of the pairs to anchor them together for stitching. Sew around the perimeter of each pinned unit, using a ¼″ seam allowance.

Pin diagonally in corners.

4. Use a rotary cutter and an acrylic ruler to cut each sewn pair in half diagonally *twice* to yield four layered triangles. Press the seam allowance of each layered triangle toward the corner with two horizontal rectangles. Use a rotary cutter and an acrylic ruler to trim each unit to 2⅛″ square, removing the dog-ear

points in the same step. You now have 24 pieced block quadrants.

Cut units diagonally into quarters.

5. Lay out four block quadrants featuring different prints in two horizontal rows as shown. Join the quadrants in each row. Press the seams of each row in opposite directions. Join the rows. Press the seam allowances to one side. Repeat with the remaining blocks quadrants to piece a total of six Patchwork blocks measuring 3¾″ square, including the seam allowances.

Make 6 blocks, 3¾″ × 3¾″.

Coffee Break

Finished quilt size: 14″ × 17¼″ ◆ Finished block size: 3¼″ × 3¼″

Designed and pieced by Kim Diehl. Machine quilted by Connie Tabor.

PIECING THE QUILT CENTER

Lay out the patchwork blocks in three horizontal rows of two blocks, turning one block in each row so the center seams alternate and will nest together. Join the blocks in each row. Press the seam allowances of each row in alternating directions. Join the rows. Press the row seam allowances to one side, or open, choosing the option that produces the best points. The pieced quilt center should measure 7″ × 10¼″, including the seam allowances.

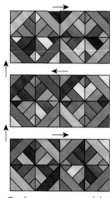

Quilt center assembly

PIECING AND ADDING BORDER #1

1. Use a pencil and an acrylic ruler to draw a diagonal sewing line from corner to corner on the wrong side of 24 of the assorted-print 1½″ squares from the border #1 patchwork set.

2. Layer a prepared 1½″ square onto one end of a cream 1½″ × 2½″ rectangle as shown. Stitch the pair together along the drawn diagonal line. Fold the resulting inner triangle open, aligning the corner with the corner of the cream rectangles. Press. Trim away the layers beneath the top triangle, leaving a ¼″ seam allowance. In the same manner add a mirror-image triangle to the remaining end of the rectangle. Repeat to piece a total of 12 flying geese units measuring 1½″ × 2½″, including the seam allowances.

Make 12 units, 1½″ × 2½″.

3. Choose four flying geese units and one print rectangle, 1½″ × 2¼″, from the border #1 patchwork set. Referring to the illustration, lay out and join the pieces. Press the seam allowances in the direction that produces the best points. Repeat to piece a total of two side border strips measuring 1½″ × 10¼″, including the seam allowances.

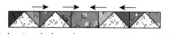

Make 2 side border strips, 1½″ × 10¼″.

4. Choose two flying geese units, two print 1½″ squares, and two print rectangles, 1½″ × 1¾″, from the border #1 patchwork set. Using the illustration as a guide, lay out and join the pieces. Press the seam allowances in the direction that produces the best points. Repeat to piece a total of two top/bottom border strips measuring 1½″ × 9″, including the seam allowances.

Make 2 top/bottom border strips, 1½″ × 9″.

5. Referring to the quilt assembly diagram, join the side border strips to the right and left sides of the quilt center. Press. Join the top and bottom border strips to the top and bottom edges of the quilt center. Press. The quilt top with border #1 should now measure 9″ × 12¼″, including the seam allowances.

Quilt assembly

ADDING BORDERS #2–#4

1. Sew a dusty aqua 1¼″ × 12¼″ strip to the right and left sides of the quilt top. Press the seam allowances toward the aqua strips. Sew a dusty aqua 1¼″ × 10½″ strip to the remaining top and bottom edges of the quilt top. Press the seam allowances toward the aqua strips.

2. Join a cream ¾″ × 13¾″ strip to the right and left sides of the quilt top. Press the seam allowances toward the cream strips. Join a cream ¾″ × 12″ strip to the remaining top and bottom edges of the quilt top. Press the seam allowances toward the cream strips.

3. Join a cranberry 2″ × 14¼″ strip to the right and left sides of the quilt top. Press the seam allowances toward the cranberry strips. Join a cranberry 2″ × 14″ strip to the remaining top and bottom edges of the quilt top. Press the seam allowances toward the cranberry strips.

COMPLETING THE QUILT

Layer and baste the quilt top, batting, and backing. Quilt the layers. The featured quilt is machine quilted with an edge-to-edge scalloped clamshell design. Join the dusty aqua binding strips to make one length and use it to bind the quilt.

Heartstrings

Does the thought of appliqué make you feel a bit hesitant? Then say hello to the: Easiest. Appliqué. Blocks. Ever. Gentle half-moon shapes are incredibly easy to master if you're new to appliqué, and, when combined with scrapaliscious patchwork blocks where only the center seams need to be matched up, the only thing easier than stitching this little lovey is living with it.

MATERIALS

Yardage is based on a 42" width of useable fabric after prewashing and removing selvages.

+ 1 fat quarter (18" × 21") of medium blue floral for patchwork, appliqué, and binding

+ 24 chubby sixteenths (9" × 10½") of assorted prints for patchwork and appliqué

+ 5 chubby sixteenths of assorted cream prints for patchwork

+ 1 yard of fabric for backing

+ 32" × 32" square of batting

+ Freezer paper for appliqué

+ Fabric glue, water-soluble and acid-free, in liquid and stick form for appliqué

+ Supplies for your favorite appliqué method

CUTTING

Cut all pieces across the width of the fabric in the order given unless otherwise noted. Instructions for cutting appliqués for my invisible machine appliqué method beginning on page 121, or you can substitute your own favorite method. The appliqué pattern is on page 37.

From the medium blue floral, cut:
1 strip, 5½" × 21"; crosscut into:
  1 square, 5½" × 5½"
  2 binding strips, 2½" × 15½"*
4 binding strips, 2½" × 21"*
Reserve the remainder of the medium blue floral print for patchwork.

From the 24 assorted prints and the remainder of the medium blue floral, cut a *combined* total of:
11 squares, 5½" × 5½" (appliqué block foundations)
117 squares, 1½" × 1½"

52 rectangles, 1½" × 2½"
48 appliqués

From the 5 assorted cream prints, cut a *combined* total of:
52 squares, 2½" × 2½"
For my chubby binding method on page 126, reduce the strip width to 2".

PIECING THE PATCHWORK BLOCKS

Sew all pieces with right sides together using a ¼″ seam allowance unless otherwise noted. Press the seam allowances as indicated by the arrows or otherwise specified.

1. Use a pencil and an acrylic ruler to draw a diagonal sewing line from corner to corner on the wrong side of 104 of the assorted-print 1½″ squares. Reserve the remaining 13 assorted-print 1½″ squares for later use.

2. Choosing the prints randomly, select two prepared print 1½″ squares and layer them onto two opposite corners of a cream 2½″ square as shown. Stitch the squares along the drawn diagonal lines. Fold the resulting inner triangles open, aligning the corners with the corners of the cream square. Press. Trim away the layers beneath the top triangles, leaving ¼″ seam allowances. Repeat to piece a total of 52 corner units measuring 2½″ square, including the seam allowances.

Make 52 units, 2½″ × 2½″

3. Lay out four corner units, four print 1½″ × 2½″ rectangles, and one of the reserved print 1½″ squares in three horizontal rows. Join the pieces in each row. Press. Join the rows. Press. Repeat to piece a total of 13 patchwork blocks measuring 5½″ square, including the seam allowances.

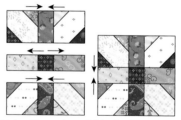

Make 13 patchwork blocks, 5½″ × 5½″.

FINISHED QUILT SIZE: 25½″ × 25½″ ◆ **FINISHED BLOCK SIZE: 5″ × 5″**

Designed, pieced, and machine appliquéd by Kim Diehl. Machine quilted by Connie Tabor.

STITCHING THE APPLIQUÉ BLOCKS

1. Referring to "Pressing Appliqué Seam Allowances" on page 123, or using your own favorite method, prepare the appliqués for stitching. Please note that only the curved applique edges should be turned under and pressed, leaving the ¼" seam allowance on the straight edge unpressed and intact.

2. Select one of the 5½" squares from the 11 assorted-print and medium blue floral squares. Choosing prints that complement each other, select four prepared appliqués. With right sides together, fold the 5½" square in half and use a hot, dry iron to lightly press a center vertical crease. Unfold the square and repeat to press a center horizontal crease. Fold each appliqué in half, right sides together, and finger-press the center crease.

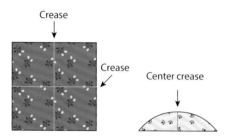

3. Align the center crease of an appliqué with the pressed crease of the foundation square on one side, positioning the appliqué so the raw straight edges are flush. Baste or pin the appliqué in place. (For my glue-basting technique that prevents shifting of the appliqués during the stitching process, see "Basting Appliqués" on page 123.) Repeat to position an appliqué onto each side of the foundation square.

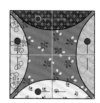

Position appliqués for stitching; pin or baste in place.

4. Referring to "Stitching the Appliqués" on page 124, or using your own favorite method, stitch the appliqués in place. Remove the freezer-paper pattern pieces, if used. To remove excess bulk, I recommend trimming away the foundation fabric beneath each appliqué, leaving a ¼" seam allowance.

5. Repeat steps 2–4 to stitch 13 appliqué blocks measuring 5½" square, including the seam allowances.

Make 13 appliqué blocks, 5½" × 5½".

PIECING THE QUILT TOP

1. Lay out three patchwork blocks and two appliqué blocks in alternating positions. Join the blocks. Press. Repeat to piece a total of three A rows measuring 5½" × 25½", including the seam allowances.

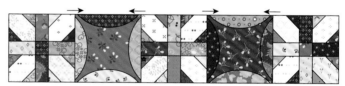

Make 3 A rows, 5½" × 25½".

2. Lay out three appliqué blocks and two patchwork blocks in alternating positions. Join the blocks. Press. Repeat to piece a total of two B rows measuring 5½" × 25½", including the seam allowances.

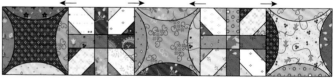

Make 2 B rows, 5½" × 25½".

3. Using the quilt pictured on page 35 as a guide, lay out the A and B rows in alternating positions. Join the rows. Press the seam allowances open.

COMPLETING THE QUILT

Layer and baste the quilt top, batting, and backing. Quilt the layers. The featured quilt is machine quilted with edge-to-edge swirls of feathered clusters. Join the medium blue floral binding strips to make one length and use it to bind the quilt.

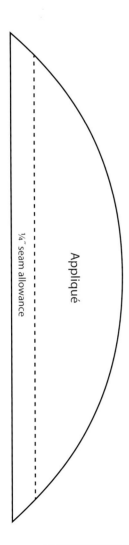

¼" seam allowance

Appliqué

Pattern does not include seam allowance except where indication. Place pattern along straight grain of fabric or in any way you choose to make the best use of your print and size of your scraps.

Garden Trug

It's been said that quilting makes the quilt, but having a strong patchwork foundation and adding a little touch of appliqué can lay the groundwork for a fabulous finish! Choosing dramatically-colored prints with a sprinkling of jewel tones helps create a sense of movement in the inviting lattice design, and the petite project size means that this little gem can be tucked into any small space.

MATERIALS

Yardage is based on a 42″ width of useable fabric after prewashing and removing selvages.

+ 1 fat quarter (18″ × 21″) of medium green print for patchwork, appliqués, and binding

+ 1 chubby sixteenth (9″ × 10½″) of dark green stripe or print for patchwork and appliqués

+ 3 bitty bricks (4½″ × 10½″) of assorted green prints for patchwork and appliqués

+ 1 chubby sixteenth of pink print for patchwork and appliqués

+ 1 bitty brick of red print for patchwork and appliqués

+ 19 charm squares (5″ × 5″) of assorted prints for patchwork

+ 1 fat eighth *each* of coordinating gray print #1 for patchwork and appliqué backgrounds and gray print #2 for patchwork

+ ⅜ yard of fabric for backing

+ 13″ × 23″ piece of batting

+ Freezer paper for appliqués

+ Fabric glue, water-soluble and acid-free, in liquid and stick form for appliqués

+ Supplies for your favorite appliqué method

CUTTING AND PREPARING THE APPLIQUÉS

The steps that follow outline cutting and preparing the shapes for my invisible machine appliqué method beginning on page 121, or you can substitute your own favorite method. Appliqué pattern is on page 43.

1. To ensure you have the patchwork pieces needed for the blocks, cut one 2⅞″ square from each of the five green prints, taking care to leave as much remaining fabric as possible. Cut each square in half diagonally *once* to yield two triangles (combined total of 10); set the green triangles aside for later use. Reserve the remainder of the green prints for the appliqué steps that follow.

2. From the remainder of the dark green print, cut four strips, 1¼″ × 10½″.

3. From the remainder of the medium green fat quarter, cut two strips, 1¼″ × 10½″.

4. From the remainder of *each* of two medium green prints, cut one strip, 1¼″ × 10½″ (combined total of 2). Please note that the remainder of the fifth green print will be used for the blossom base appliqués.

5. For the pieced strips that the leaf appliqués will be cut from, join the previously cut green strips in pairs along the long edges, with one dark green strip used in each pair. Press the seam allowances open.

6. Use a pencil to trace each appliqué shape the number of times specified below onto the non-waxy side of freezer paper, and cut out each shape exactly along the drawn lines:

Outer blossom: 2
Inner blossom: 2
Blossom base: 2
Leaf: 4 and 4 reversed, including the dashed center line for pattern-piece placement in the next step.

7. Apply a small dab of glue stick to the center of the non-waxy side one leaf and one reversed leaf pattern piece; position these pieces onto the wrong side of a pieced green strip from step 5, aligning the dashed lines with the center seam and leaving about 1″ of space between each. Repeat with the remaining leaf pattern pieces and pieced green strips. Cut out each leaf, adding an approximate ¼″ seam allowance.

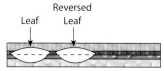

Cut a total of 4 leaves and 4 reversed leaves.

8. Referring to "Preparing Appliqués from Fabric" on page 122 (or substituting your own favorite method), cut two *each* of the blossom bases from the reserved remainder of the fifth green print, inner blossoms from the chubby sixteenth of pink print, and outer blossoms from the bitty brick of red print.

9. Referring to "Pressing Appliqué Seam Allowances" on page 123 (or substituting your own favorite method), press all cut appliqués to finish the edges and prepare them for stitching. It isn't necessary to finish the bottom raw end of the blossom bases, as they'll be enclosed within the seam allowances when the table topper is pieced. Reserve all of the prepared appliqués, as well as the scraps of appliqué prints, for later use.

CUTTING FOR THE REMAINDER OF THE TABLE RUNNER

Cut all pieces across the width of the fabric in the order given unless otherwise noted.

From the charm squares, and the remainder of the prints used for the appliqués, cut a *combined* total of:
20 squares, 2⅞″ × 2⅞″; cut each square in half diagonally *once* to yield 2 triangles (combined total of 40, grand total of 50 with previously cut triangles). **Note:** For a scrappier look in my project, I cut an extra handful of squares and discarded the unused triangles after completing the patchwork.

From gray print #1, cut:
1 strip, 1¾″ × 21″; crosscut into 11 squares, 1¾″ × 1¾″
1 strip, 2½″ × 21″; from this strip, cut:
  4 squares, 2½″ × 2½″
  1 square, 1¾″ × 1¾″ (total of 12 with the previously cut squares)
1 strip, 3½″ × 21″; crosscut into 2 rectangles, 3½″ × 8½″

From gray print #2, cut:
3 strips, 1¾″ × 21″; crosscut into 28 squares, 1¾″ × 1¾″

From the reserved remainder of the fat quarter of green print, cut:
4 binding strips, 2½″ × 21″ (For my chubby binding method on page 126, reduce the strip width to 2″.)

Garden Trug

Finished quilt size: 8½″ × 18½″ ◆ Finished block size: 2½″ × 2½″

Designed, pieced, and machine appliquéd by Kim Diehl. Machine quilted by Connie Tabor.

PIECING THE CENTER UNIT OF THE TABLE RUNNER

Sew all pieces with right sides together using a ¼″ seam allowance unless otherwise noted. Press the seam allowances as indicated by the arrows or otherwise specified.

1. Choosing prints that work well together, join two assorted-print 2⅞″ triangles along the long diagonal edges. Press. Trim away the dog-ear points. Repeat to piece a total of 20 half-square-triangle units measuring 2½″ square, including the seam allowances.

Make 20 half-square-triangle units, 2½″ × 2½″.

★ **EXTRA SNIPPET** ★

Triangle Trick

No matter how carefully I cut my patchwork pieces, especially triangles, when I layer them together for stitching, they'll sometimes be slightly different in size. When this happens, I've learned to align the back corners opposite the long diagonal edges for the piecing step. This layering approach ensures that any difference in triangle size will be absorbed into the seam allowance along the long diagonal edge as the unit is stitched. Give this little trick a try—it works!

---

2. Use a pencil and an acrylic ruler to draw a diagonal sewing line from corner to corner on the wrong side of all gray 1¾″ squares. Keep the prepared gray #1 and gray #2 squares in separate sets.

3. Using the gray #2 squares, layer a prepared 1¾″ square into one corner of a pieced half-square-triangle unit from step 1 as shown. Stitch the pair together along the drawn diagonal line. Fold the resulting inner gray triangle open, aligning it with the corner of the half-square-triangle unit. Press. Trim away the layers beneath the top triangle, leaving a ¼″ seam allowance. Repeat using the remaining half-square-triangle units to make a total of 20 partial block units measuring 2½″ square, including the seam allowances.

Make 20 partial block units, 2½″ × 2½″.

4. Choose eight partial block units. Using the remaining prepared gray #2 squares, repeat step 3 to add a mirror-image triangle to the open corner of each unit, opposite the first gray triangle to complete eight A blocks measuring 2½″ square, including the seam allowances.

Make 8 A blocks, 2½″ × 2½″.

5. Add a gray #1 triangle to the open corner of the remaining partial block units as described in step 4 to complete 12 B blocks measuring 2½″ square, including the seam allowances.

Make 12 B blocks, 2½″ × 2½″.

6. Referring to the illustration for placement of the A and B blocks and the orientation of the gray #1 and #2 prints, lay out the completed blocks and four 2½″ gray #1 squares in six horizontal rows as shown. Join the pieces in each row. Press. Join the rows. Press. The pieced center unit should measure 8½″ × 12½″, including the seam allowances.

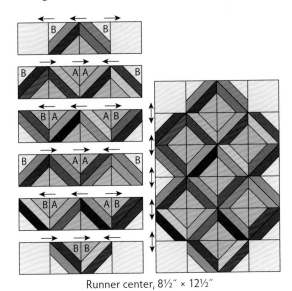

Runner center, 8½″ × 12½″

ADDING THE APPLIQUÉD END PIECES

1. Fold the gray #1 rectangles in half crosswise, right sides together, and use a hot, dry iron to lightly press a center crease. Fold each prepared blossom base, inner blossom, and outer blossom in half and finger press a vertical center crease in each.

2. Referring to "Basting Appliqués" on page 123, work from the bottom layer to the top to position and baste the blossom design onto each gray #1 rectangle, using the pressed creases to center the shapes. Ensure the raw blossom base edges are aligned with the raw edge of the background rectangles, and they'll be enclosed within the seam allowances when the table runner is pieced together. Referring to "Stitching the Appliqués" on page 124 (or substituting your own favorite method), work from the bottom layer to the top to stitch the blossom appliqués in place. Make two appliquéd rectangles.

Lay out design and stitch appliqués, starting with the bottom layer.

3. Using the quilt pictured on page 41 as a guide, join an appliquéd blossom gray #1 rectangle to each short end of the table runner center unit. Press the seam allowances toward the table runner center unit.

4. Referring again to the photo on page 41, position four leaves at each end of the table runner and stitch in place.

COMPLETING THE QUILT

Layer and baste the quilt top, batting, and backing. Quilt the layers. The featured quilt is machine quilted with an edge-to-edge chicken wire design. Join the medium green binding strips to make one length and use it to bind the quilt.

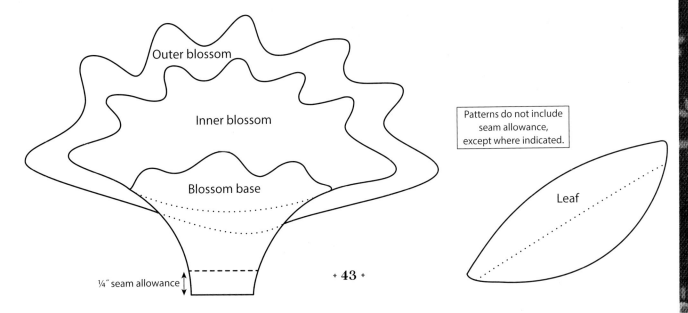

Outer blossom

Inner blossom

Blossom base

Leaf

Patterns do not include seam allowance, except where indicated.

¼″ seam allowance

In and Out

Once in a while, the best and most fun-to-stitch quilt blocks can be the result of a happy accident. What started out as a Star block with (oops!) incorrectly placed star-point units, inspired the patchwork blocks in this mini. With an open mind, sometimes things that seem to go very wrong can be the start of something incredibly right!

MATERIALS

Yardage is based on a 42″ width of useable fabric after prewashing and removing selvages.

- 1 fat quarter (18″ × 21″) of black print for patchwork and binding
- 24 squares, 6″ × 6″, of assorted prints (collectively referred to as "darks") for patchwork
- 5 fat eighths (9″ × 21″) of assorted cream prints for patchwork and border
- 1 fat quarter of fabric for backing
- 18″ × 18″ square of batting

CUTTING

Cut all pieces across the width of the fabric in the order given unless otherwise noted. For added versatility when stitching the patchwork, you may wish to cut a small handful of pieces in each given size as your fabrics permit.

From the black fat quarter, cut:
4 binding strips, 2½″ × 21″ (for my chubby binding method on page 126, reduce the stitch width to 2″)

From the 24 assorted prints and the remainder of the black print (collectively referred to as "darks"), cut a *combined* total of:
72 squares, 1½″ × 1½″
18 rectangles, 1½″ × 2½″

From the 5 assorted cream prints, cut a *combined* total of:
2 strips, 1¼″ × 12½″
2 strips, 1¼″ × 14″
9 squares, 2½″ × 2½″
72 squares, 1½″ × 1½″
18 rectangles, 1½″ × 2½″

PIECING THE IN AND OUT PATCHWORK BLOCKS

Sew all pieces with right sides together using a ¼″ seam allowance unless otherwise noted. Press the seam allowances as indicated by the arrows or otherwise specified.

1. Use a pencil and an acrylic ruler to draw a diagonal sewing line from corner to corner on the wrong side of the 72 dark 1½″ squares and 36 of the cream 1½″ squares. Set the prepared cream squares aside for later use.

2. Choosing the prints randomly, select four prepared dark squares. Layer a prepared square onto two opposite corners of a cream 2½″ square as shown. Stitch the squares together along the drawn diagonal lines. Fold the resulting inner triangles open, aligning the corners with the corners of the cream square. Press. Trim away the layers beneath the top triangles, leaving ¼″ seam allowances. In the same manner, use the remaining two dark squares to add stitched triangles to the remaining corners of the cream square. Repeat to piece a total of nine square-in-a-square units measuring 2½″ square, including the seam allowances.

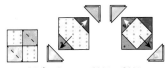

Make 9 units, 2½″ × 2½″.

3. Again choosing the prints randomly, select two prepared dark squares from step 1. Stitch a square to one end of a cream 1½″ × 2½″ rectangle as instructed in step 2. Then sew a second dark square to the other end of the cream rectangle to add a mirror-

image triangle. Repeat to piece a total of 18 cream-background star-point units measuring 1½″ × 2½″, including the seam allowances.

Make 18 cream-background units, 1½″ × 2½″.

4. Repeat step 3 using the prepared cream squares and the dark 1½″ × 2½″ rectangles to piece 18 dark-background star-point units measuring 1½″ × 2½″.

Make 18 dark-background units, 1½″ × 2½″.

5. Lay out one square-in-a-square unit, two cream-background star-point units, two dark-background star-point units, and four assorted cream 1½″ squares in three horizontal rows as shown. Join the pieces in each row. Press. Join the rows. Press. Repeat to piece a total of nine In and Out blocks measuring 4½″ square, including the seam allowances.

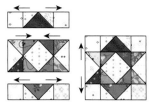

Make 9 blocks, 4½″ × 4½″.

ASSEMBLING THE QUILT TOP

1. Lay out the nine pieced In and Out blocks in three horizontal rows, rotating the blocks as shown. Join the blocks in each row. Press. Join the rows. Press. The quilt center should measure 12½″ square, including the seam allowances.

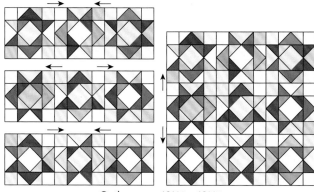

Quilt center, 12½″ × 12½″

2. Join the cream 1¼″ × 12½″ strips to the right and left sides of the quilt center. Press the seam allowances toward the cream strips. Join the cream 1¼″ × 14″ strips to the top and bottom edges of the quilt center. Press. The completed quilt top should measure 14″ × 14″.

COMPLETING THE QUILT

Layer and baste the quilt top, batting, and backing. Quilt the layers. The featured quilt is machine quilted with an edge-to-edge chicken wire design. Join the black binding strips to make one length and use it to bind the quilt.

FINISHED QUILT SIZE: 14″ × 14″ ♦ FINISHED BLOCK SIZE: 4″ × 4″

Designed and pieced by Kim Diehl. Machine quilted by Connie Tabor.

Hog Tied

Pull out your favorite quilting prints and forget about the perfect little black dress, all you really need when you want to feel special is a handful of perfect little bow ties. Add a twisty pieced border that only looks complicated, and you've got one captivating mini that's all dressed up and ready to mingle.

MATERIALS

Yardage is based on a 42″ width of useable fabric after prewashing and removing selvages.

- 1 fat quarter (18″ × 21″) of cream print for patchwork
- 4 chubby sixteenths (9″ × 10½″) of assorted cream prints for patchwork
- 1 fat eighth (9″ × 21″) of medium green print for patchwork
- 23 charm squares (5″ × 5″) of assorted prints for patchwork
- ½ yard of black print for patchwork and binding
- ⅔ yard of fabric for backing
- 24″ × 24″ square of batting

CUTTING

Cut all pieces across the width of the fabric in the order given unless otherwise noted. WOF is defined as width of fabric. For added versatility when stitching the patchwork, you may wish to cut a small handful of pieces in each given size as your fabrics permit.

From the cream print, cut:
1 strip, 3¼″ × 21″; crosscut into 6 squares, 3¼″ × 3¼″. Cut each square in half diagonally *once* to yield 4 triangles (total of 24).
4 strips, 1″ × 21″; crosscut into 4 strips, 1″ × 12½″
Reserve the remainder of the cream print.

From the medium green print, cut:
2 strips, 2⅞″ × 21″; crosscut into 12 squares, 2⅞″ × 2⅞″. Cut each square in half diagonally *once* to yield 2 triangles (total of 24).
Reserve the remainder of the medium green print.

From the dark charm squares and the remaining medium green print, cut 36 dark patchwork sets of matching squares:
2 squares, 1½″ × 1½″
2 squares, 1″ × 1″
Keep matching squares together in sets of 2 small and 2 larger squares.

From the black print, cut:
2 strips, 1″ × WOF; crosscut into 4 strips, 1″ × 12½″
1 strip, 3½″ × WOF; crosscut into:
  4 squares, 3½″ × 3½″
  6 squares, 3¼″ × 3¼″; cut each square in half diagonally *twice* to yield 4 triangles (total of 24)
2 binding strips, 2½″ × 42″ (For my chubby binding method on page 126, reduce the strip width to 2″.)

From the 4 cream chubby sixteenths and the reserved remainder of the cream fat quarter, cut:
36 pairs of matching squares, 1½″ × 1½″ (72 total; keep matching prints together)

Piecing the Bow Tie Blocks

Sew all pieces with right sides together using a ¼″ seam allowance unless otherwise noted. Press the seam allowances as indicated by the arrows or other specified.

1. Select one dark and one light patchwork set. Use a pencil and an acrylic ruler to draw a diagonal sewing line from corner to corner on the wrong side of the two dark 1″ squares.

2. Layer a prepared dark square onto one corner of a light 1½″ square. Stitch the pair along the drawn diagonal line. Press the resulting inner dark triangle open, aligning the corner with the corner of the light square. Trim away the layers beneath the top triangle, leaving a ¼″ seam allowance. Repeat to make a total of two pieced squares measuring 1½″ square, including the seam allowances.

Make 2 pieced squares, 1½″ × 1½″.

3. Lay out the two pieced squares and two dark matching-print 1½″ squares in two horizontal rows as shown. Join the squares in each row. Press. Join the rows. Press. The pieced Bow Tie block should measure 2½″ square, including the seam allowances.

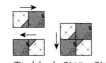

Bow Tie block, 2½″ × 2½″

4. Repeat steps 1–3 to piece a total of 36 Bow Tie blocks.

FINISHED QUILT SIZE: 18½″ × 18½″ ♦ FINISHED BLOCK SIZE: 2″ × 2″

Designed by Kim Diehl. Pieced by Jennifer Martinez. Machine quilted by Connie Tabor.

PIECING THE QUILT CENTER

1. Lay out six Bow Tie blocks, rotating every other block so the center seam allowances rest in opposite directions and will nest together. Join the blocks. Press. Repeat to piece a total of six block rows measuring 2½″ × 12½″, including the seam allowances.

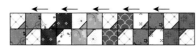

Make 6 block rows, 2½″ × 12½″.

2. Lay out the six block rows, alternating the direction of every other row so the block seams will nest together. Join the rows. Press. The pieced quilt center should measure 12½″ square, including the seam allowances.

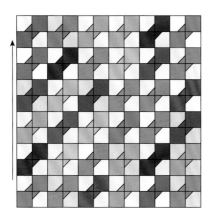

Pieced quilt center, 12½″ × 12½″

PIECING AND ADDING THE BORDER

1. Join a cream and a black triangle as shown. Press. Trim away the dog-ear points. Repeat to sew a total of 24 pieced triangles.

Make 24 pieced triangles.

2. Layer a green triangle onto a pieced triangle from step 1. Join the pair along the long diagonal edges. Press. Trim away the dog-ear points. Repeat to piece a total of 24 Half-Square-Triangle Variation blocks measuring 2½″ square, including the seam allowances.

Make 24 Half-Square-Triangle Variation blocks, 2½″ × 2½″.

3. Lay out six Half-Square-Triangle Variation blocks, rotating every other block as shown to form the border design. Join the blocks. Press. Repeat to piece a total of four border strips, 2½″ × 12½″, including the seam allowances.

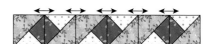

Make 4 border strips, 2½″ × 12½″.

4. Join a black 1″ × 12½″ strip to one long edge of each pieced border strip and a cream 1″ × 12½″ strip to the other long edge as shown. Press. Repeat to complete four border units measuring 3½″ × 12½″, including the seam allowances.

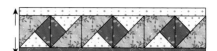

Make 4 border units, 3½″ × 12½″.

5. Referring to the assembly diagram, join a completed border unit to the right and left sides of the quilt center. Press. Join a black 3½″ square to each end of the remaining two border units. Press. Join these pieced borders to the remaining sides of the quilt center. Press.

Quilt assembly

COMPLETING THE QUILT

Layer and baste the quilt top, batting, and backing. Quilt the layers. The featured quilt is machine quilted with an edge-to-edge orange peel design. Join the black binding strips to make one length and use it to bind the quilt.

Written in the Stars

Stitch sparkling stars in rich shades of navy and teal, surround them with patches of apple green, and you've got yourself a mini that's quite comfortable being in the spotlight. If my three chosen colors don't tickle your fancy, simply pick your three favorite colors, and tailor this quilt to showcase your own special style.

MATERIALS

Yardage is based on a 42″ width of useable fabric after prewashing and removing selvages.

+ ⅜ yard of teal print for blocks and border
+ ⅝ yard of navy print for blocks, border, and binding
+ ⅜ yard of apple-green print for blocks and border
+ ¼ yard (not a fat quarter) of cream print for blocks and border
+ ⅜ yard of beige print for blocks and border
+ ¾ yard of fabric for backing
+ 27″ × 27″ square of batting

CUTTING

Cut all pieces across the width of the fabric in the order given unless otherwise noted. WOF is defined as width of fabric.

From the teal print, cut:
1 strip, 3¼″ × WOF; from this strip, cut:
  4 squares, 3¼″ × 3¼″; cut each square in half diagonally *twice* to yield 4 triangles (total of 16)
  4 squares, 3″ × 3″; cut each square in half diagonally *once* to yield 2 triangles (total of 8)
  6 squares, 2½″ × 2½″
1 strip, 1½″ × WOF; crosscut into 22 squares,
    1½″ × 1½″

From the navy print, cut:
1 strip, 3¼″ × WOF; from this strip, cut:
  4 squares, 3¼″ × 3¼″; cut each square in half diagonally *twice* to yield 4 triangles (total of 16)

4 squares, 3″ × 3″; cut each square in half diagonally *once* to yield 2 triangles (total of 8)
6 squares, 2½″ × 2½″
1 strip, 1½″ × WOF; crosscut into 22 squares,
    1½″ × 1½″
3 binding strips, 2½″ × 42″. (For Kim's chubby binding method on page 126, reduce the strip width to 2″.)

From the apple-green print, cut:
3 strips, 1½″ × WOF; crosscut into:
  56 squares, 1½″ × 1½″
  8 rectangles, 1½″ × 2½″
2 strips, 2½″ × WOF; crosscut into 24 squares,
    2½″ × 2½″

From the cream print, cut:
1 strip, 3¼″ × WOF; from this strip, cut:
  8 squares, 3¼″ × 3¼″; cut each square in half diagonally *twice* to yield 4 triangles (total of 32)
  5 squares, 1½″ × 1½″
1 strip, 1½″ × WOF; crosscut into 27 squares,
    1½″ × 1½″ (total of 32 with previously cut squares)

From the beige print, cut:
1 strip, 3″ × WOF; from this strip, cut:
  8 squares, 3″ × 3″; cut each square in half diagonally *once* to yield 2 triangles (total of 16)
  5 squares, 1½″ × 1½″
1 strip, 1½″ × WOF; crosscut into 27 squares,
    1½″ × 1½″ (total of 32 with previously cut squares)
1 strip, 3½″ × WOF; crosscut into 8 rectangles,
    3½″ × 4½″
1 strip 2½″ × WOF; crosscut into 8 rectangles,
    2½″ × 3½″

PIECING THE STAR BLOCKS

Sew all pieces with right sides together using a ¼″ seam allowance unless otherwise noted. Press the seam allowances as indicated by the arrows or otherwise specified.

1. Select 16 teal and 16 cream 3¼″ triangles. Lay out two teal and 2 cream triangles in two diagonal rows as shown. Join the triangles in each row. Press. Trim away the dog-ear points. Join the two diagonal rows. Press. Trim away the dog-ear points. Repeat to piece a total of eight hourglass units measuring 2½″ square, including the seam allowances.

Make 8 hourglass units, 2½″ × 2½″.

+ EXTRA SNIPPET +

Perfectly-Sized Hourglass Units

The triangle measurements provided for the hourglass units in this quilt are mathematically correct, but experience has taught me that individual seam allowance differences can produce finished units that may differ slightly in size. My favorite way to compensate for this variable is to use a *slightly* scant ¼″ seam allowance as I stitch the triangles, producing a unit that's slightly oversized. Once the unit is pieced and pressed, I use a rotary cutter and a small acrylic ruler featuring a center diagonal line to trim away the slight excess bit of fabric on each side of the unit. This approach eliminates the need to cut the pieces larger than needed, which would result in waste, and the trimming step produces perfectly sized patchwork every time!

---

2. Join an apple-green 1½″ × 2½″ rectangle to one cream side of each hourglass unit. Press. The completed units should measure 2½″ × 3½″, including the seam allowances.

Make 8 hourglass patchwork units, 2½″ × 3½″.

3. Select eight beige and eight navy 3″ triangles. Join a beige and a navy triangle along the long diagonal edges. Press. Use a rotary cutter and an acrylic ruler to trim the unit on all sides so it is 2½″ square. Repeat to piece a total of eight half-square-triangle units.

Make 8 half-square-triangle units, 2½″ × 2½″.

4. Choose eight each of the beige, apple-green, and cream 1½″ squares. Join three squares, one in each color, as shown. Press. Repeat to piece a total of eight three-square units measuring 1½″ × 3½″, including the seam allowances.

Make 8 three-square units, 1½″ × 3½″.

FINISHED QUILT SIZE: 22½″ × 22½″

Designed and pieced by Kim Diehl. Machine quilted by Connie Tabor.

5. Choose eight additional beige and eight additional apple-green 1½" squares. Join the squares in pairs as shown. Press. Repeat to piece a total of eight two-square units measuring 1½" × 2½", including the seam allowances.

Make 8 two-square units, 1½" × 2½".

6. Select the eight two-square units, the eight half-square-triangle units from step 3, and the eight three-square units from step 4. Join the beige side of a half-square-triangle unit to a two-square unit as shown. Press. Join a three-square unit to the pieced half-square-triangle unit as shown. Press. Repeat to piece a total of four corner units and four mirror-image corner units measuring 3½" square, including the seam allowances.

Make 4 corner units and 4 mirror-image corner units, 3½" × 3½".

7. Lay out two corner units and two mirror-image corner units, four hourglass-patchwork units from step 2, and one navy 2½" square in three horizontal rows as shown. Join the pieces in each row. Press. Join

the rows. Press. Repeat to piece a total of two teal Star blocks with navy centers, measuring 8½" square including the seam allowances.

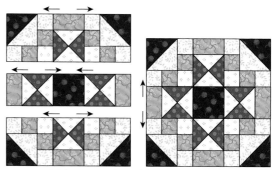

Make two teal Star blocks, 8½" × 8½".

8. Substituting the navy 3¼" triangles, the teal 3" triangles, and the teal 2½" square for the dark colors used in the teal Star blocks, repeat steps 1–7 to piece two navy Star blocks with teal centers, measuring 8½" square, including the seam allowances.

Make 2 navy Star blocks, 8½" × 8½".

PIECING THE QUILT CENTER

Referring to the illustration, lay out the two teal Star blocks and the two navy Star blocks in two horizontal rows as shown. Join the blocks in each row. Press. Join the rows. Press. The pieced quilt center should measure 16½″ square, including the seam allowances.

Quilt center, 16½″ × 16½″

PIECING AND ADDING THE BORDER

1. Select eight beige 2½″ × 4½″ rectangles, four navy 2½″ squares, four teal 2½″ squares, and 24 apple-green 2½″ squares. Use a pencil and an acrylic ruler to draw a diagonal sewing line from corner to corner on the wrong side of each of squares.

2. Layer a prepared apple-green square and a prepared navy square onto opposite ends of a beige 2½″ × 4½″ rectangle as shown. Stitch the squares to the rectangle along the drawn diagonal lines. Fold the resulting inner triangles open, aligning the corners with the corners of the beige rectangle. Press. Trim away the layers beneath the top triangles, leaving ¼″ seam allowances. Repeat using the remaining beige rectangles and prepared squares to make two each of the regular and mirror-image units shown (total of 8 units), measuring

2½″ × 4½″, including the seam allowances. Reserve the remaining 16 prepared apple-green 2½″ squares for the next step.

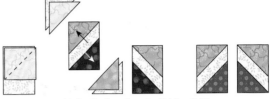

Make 2 of each unit, 2½″ × 4½″.

3. Layer a reserved prepared apple-green 2½″ square onto one corner of a beige 3½″ × 4½″ rectangle as shown. Stitch, press, and trim, as previously instructed to form a green triangle corner. In the same manner, add a mirror-image green triangle to the adjacent rectangle corner. Repeat to piece a total of eight green flying-geese units measuring 3½″ × 4½″, including the seam allowances.

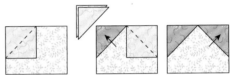

Make 8 units, 3½″ × 4½″.

4. Choose 24 apple-green 1½″ squares, 12 navy 1½″ squares, and 12 teal 1½″ squares. Lay out three green squares and three navy squares in two vertical rows as shown. Join the squares in each row. Press. Join the rows. Press. Repeat to piece a total of four green/navy checkerboard units measuring 2½″ × 3½″, including the seam allowances. In the same manner, use the remaining apple-green and teal 1½″ squares to piece a total of four green/teal checkerboard units.

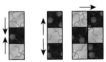

Make 4 green/navy units and 4 green/teal units, 2½″ × 4½″.

5. Referring to the illustration, lay out one each of the green/navy and green/teal checkerboard units, one each of the navy and teal patchwork units from step 2, and two of the green flying-geese units from step 3. Join the units. Press. Repeat to piece two side border row units measuring 3½″ × 16½″, including the seam allowances.

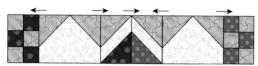

Make 2 side border units, 3½″ × 16½″.

6. Join the cream edge of each side border row unit to the right and left sides of the quilt center. Press the seam allowances away from the quilt center.

7. Repeat step 5, reversing the positions of the navy and teal prints, to piece two top/bottom border row units measuring 3½″ × 16½″, including the seam allowances. Reserve these pieced border row units to use in step 9.

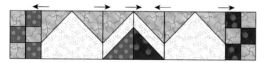

Make 2 top/bottom border units, 3½″ × 16½″.

8. Select 16 cream 1½″ squares, 10 teal 1½″ squares, and 10 navy 1½″ squares. Using four teal squares, four cream squares, and one navy square, lay out the squares in three horizontal rows as shown. Join the squares in each row. Press. Join the rows. Press. Repeat to piece a total of two teal nine-patch units measuring 3½″ square including the seam allowances. In the same manner, use the remaining squares to piece a total of two navy nine-patch units measuring 3½″ square.

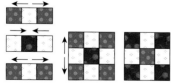

Make 2 teal and 2 navy nine-patch units, 3½″ × 3½″.

9. Referring to the quilt pictured on page 57, join a teal nine-patch unit to the teal checkerboard end of a top/bottom border unit, and a navy nine-patch unit to the navy checkerboard end of the top/bottom border unit. Press the seam allowances toward the nine-patch units. Repeat to complete two top/bottom border units. Join the beige edges of these units to the remaining sides of the quilt center. Press the seam allowances toward the newly added borders.

COMPLETING THE QUILT

Layer and baste the quilt top, batting, and backing. Quilt the layers. The featured quilt is machine quilted with an edge-to-edge repeating design of curved triangle shapes that are echo quilted within each triangle. Join the navy binding strips to make one length and use it to bind the quilt.

DON'T FORGET
To ORDER

BUTTER	SOUR CREAM
CREAM	ORANGE JUICE
DIPS	COTTAGE CHEESE
CHOC. MILK	SKIM MILK
ORANGE	BUTTER MILK
EGG	MAPLE

Cookies and Milk

Is it cookies and milk, or milk and cookies? Whether you notice the creamy background first, or the colorful pieced "cookies," the morsels and crumbs at the center of each block totally take the cake. Simple nine patches begin their journey in granny-square form, and then they're turned on point and trimmed to make for some super fun stitching time. This is one time when it's okay to double dip!

MATERIALS

Yardage is based on a 42″ width of useable fabric after prewashing and removing selvages.

- ⅜ yard of dark print for the main print of 1 block, for the border, and binding
- 8 fat eighths (9″ × 21″) of assorted prints, to be the main prints for blocks, and for the border
- 9 charm squares (5″ × 5″) of assorted prints, in colors to compliment the main block prints, and for the border

Approximately ⅓″ yard *total* of assorted-print scraps for blocks and border

- 4 fat eighths of assorted cream prints for blocks
- ⅞ yard of fabric for backing
- 31″ × 31″ square of batting

CUTTING

Cut all pieces across the width of the fabric in the order given unless otherwise noted. WOF is defined as width of fabric. For greater ease in choosing your prints, cutting for the border is provided separately, after the quilt center has been pieced.

From the dark print, cut:
3 strips, 2½″ × 42″; from one strip, cut 2 squares, 2½″ × 2½″, for the center block. Cut each square in half diagonally *once* to yield 2 triangles (total of 4). Reserve the remainder of the partially cut strip, and the other two strips, for the binding. (For my chubby binding method on page 126, reduce the strip width to 2″.)

1 strip, 2″ × WOF; from this strip, cut:
  8 squares, 2″ × 2″
  8 squares, 1½″ × 1½″
Organize the 4 triangles cut from the 2½″ squares, each of the 2″ squares, and each of the 1½″ squares into a dark block patchwork set. Reserve the remainder of the dark print for use in the border.

From *each* of the fat eighths of assorted prints (collectively referred to as "dark" from this point forward), cut:
1 strip, 2½″ × 21″; from this strip, cut 2 squares, 2½″ × 2½″ (combined total of 16). Cut each square in half diagonally *once* to yield 2 triangles (combined total of 32). From the remainder of each strip, cut 8 squares, 1½″ × 1½″ (combined total of 64).
Organize the pieces by print into 8 dark block patchwork sets (total of 9 with previously cut set). Reserve the remainder of the dark prints for use in the border.

From *each* of the 9 charm squares of assorted prints, cut:
4 squares, 1½″ × 1½″ (combined total of 36).
Organize the squares by print, adding each set of 4 squares to a complimentary dark block set.

From the scraps of assorted prints, cut a *combined* total of:
9 squares, 1½″ × 1½″. Add one square to each of the dark block patchwork sets for use as the center square.
Reserve the remainder of the assorted-print scraps for use in the border.

Continued on page 64

Continued from page 63

From *each* of the four assorted cream prints, cut:

9 rectangles, 2″ × 3½″ (combined total of 36)

5 squares, 2½″ × 2½″ (combined total of 20); cut each
    square in half diagonally *once* to yield 2 triangles
    (combined total of 40).

Organize the cream pieces by print into 9 cream block
patchwork sets, with each set consisting of 1 rectangle
from each of the four prints, and 1 triangle from each
of the four prints. You'll have one unused triangle from
each cream print.

PIECING THE BLOCK CENTER UNITS

*Sew all pieces with right sides together using a ¼″
seam allowance unless otherwise noted. Press the seam
allowances as indicated by the arrows or otherwise
specified.*

1. Select a dark block patchwork set and a cream
block patchwork set. From the dark set, choose eight
1½″ squares from the main print, four 1½″ squares
from the complimentary print, and the 1½″ square
chosen for the center square. Reserving four 1½″
main-print squares, lay out the remaining squares in
three horizontal rows as shown. Use a slightly scant
seam allowance (a couple threads less than a true ¼″)
to stitch the squares in each row. Press. Join the rows.
Press. Repeat to piece a total of nine units, a slightly
generous 3½″ × 3½″, including the seam allowances.

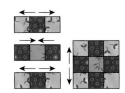

Make 9 units, a generous 3½″ × 3½″.

2. Using the four reserved main print 1½″ squares,
join a square to each side of the step 1 unit as shown.
Press. Repeat with the remaining step 1 units.

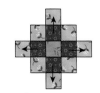

Complete 9 center units.

3. Use a rotary cutter and an acrylic ruler to trim
and square-up each block center unit to measure 3½″
square, including the seam allowances.

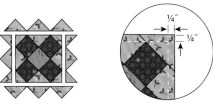

Trim center units to 3½″ × 3½″.

COMPLETING THE PATCHWORK BLOCKS

1. Use a pencil and an acrylic ruler to draw a diagonal
sewing line from corner to corner on the wrong side
of the eight dark 2″ squares in each patchwork set,
keeping the squares organized by print.

2. Choose one set of prepared dark 2″ squares and a
cream block patchwork set. Layer a prepared square
onto one end of a cream 2″ × 3½″ rectangle. Stitch the
pieces along the drawn line. Fold the resulting inner
dark triangle open, aligning the corner with the corner
of the cream rectangle. Press. Trim away the layers
beneath the top triangle, leaving a ¼″ seam allowance.
In the same manner add a mirror-image dark triangle
to the unit. Repeat to piece a total of four flying geese
units per block measuring 2″ × 3½″, including the
seam allowances.

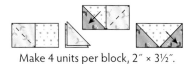

Make 4 units per block, 2″ × 3½″.

3. Using the dark and cream 2½″ triangles remaining
in the patchwork sets, join a dark and a cream triangle
along the long diagonal edges. Press. Use a rotary
cutter and an acrylic ruler to trim the unit to 2″ square,
removing the dog-ear points in the same step. Repeat
to piece a total of four half-square-triangle units per
block.

Make 4 units per block, 2″ × 2″.

Finished quilt size: 24½″ × 24½″ • **Finished block size: 6″ × 6″**

Designed and pieced by Kim Diehl. Machine quilted by Connie Tabor.

4. Lay out a pieced block center unit, four matching-print flying-geese units from step 2, and four matching-print half-square-triangle units from step 3 in three horizontal rows as shown. Join the pieces in each row. Press. Join the rows. Press. The pieced block should measure 6½" square, including the seam allowances.

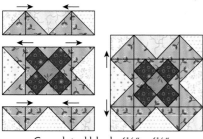

Completed block, 6½" × 6½".

5. Repeat steps 2–4 to piece a total of nine blocks.

Piecing the Quilt Center

Lay out the pieced blocks in three horizontal rows of three blocks. (I positioned my block sewn from the binding print as the center block, to create a sense of balance.) Join the blocks. Press. Join the rows. Press. The pieced quilt center should measure 18½" square, including the seam allowances.

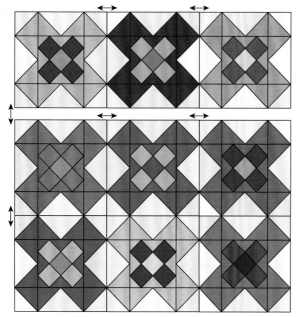

Pieced quilt center, 18½" × 18½".

Cutting, Piecing, and Adding the Border

1. From the assorted-print scraps (choosing fabrics that complement the blocks) and the reserved remainder of all dark prints, cut a *combined* total of:

16 rectangles, 1½" × 4¼"

4 rectangles, 1½" × 4"

8 rectangles, 1½" × 3¾"

8 rectangles, 1½" × 3¼"

8 rectangles, 1½" × 3"

8 rectangles, 1½" × 2¾"

8 rectangles, 1½" × 2½"

16 rectangles, 1½" × 2"

48 squares, 1½" × 1½"

2. Referring to the illustration for patchwork sizes, and positioning the prints in a way that compliments the blocks, lay out the pieces indicated in three horizontal rows. Join the pieces in each row. Press the seam allowances to one side, in any direction you choose. Join the rows. Press the seam allowances toward the top row. Repeat to piece a total of four border units measuring 3½" × 18½", including the seam allowances.

Piece 4 border units, 3½" × 18½".

3. Using the remaining assorted-print 1½" squares, sew four nine-patch units for the border corners. Press as shown. The nine-patch units should measure 3½" square, including the seam allowances.

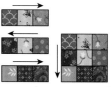

Make 4 nine-patch corner units, 3½" × 3½".

4. Join a pieced border unit from step 2 to the right and left sides of the quilt center, with the patchwork strip featuring the middle 4″-long rectangle joined to the block edges. Press the seam allowances toward the border units.

5. Join the nine-patch units from step 3 to the ends of the remaining two border units. Press the seam allowances toward the border units. Join these pieced borders to the top and bottom edges of the quilt center. Press the seam allowances toward the borders.

COMPLETING THE QUILT

Layer and baste the quilt top, batting, and backing. Quilt the layers. The featured quilt is machine quilted with an edge-to-edge design of clusters of four feathered fronds. Join the dark binding strips to make one length of binding and use it to bind the quilt.

Traffic Jam

Take the fast lane to piecing this mini by cutting a plethora of "strippies" in a range of colors and random widths, and then set aside typical quilting guidelines as you join them randomly into easygoing patchwork units. Fashion these units into simple spool shapes that seem to be wound with threads of cheer, and enjoy the sense of movement this little quilt brings.

MATERIALS

Yardage is based on a 42″ width of useable fabric after prewashing and removing selvages.

+ 28 skinny eighths (4½″ × 21″) of assorted prints for patchwork, border, and binding
+ 5 fat eighths (9″ × 21″) of assorted cream prints for patchwork
+ ⅞ yard of fabric for backing
+ 29″ × 29″ square of batting

CUTTING

Cut all pieces across the width of the fabric in the order given unless otherwise noted.

From *each* of the 28 assorted prints, cut:

1 strip, 1½″ × 4½″, across one end of the print (combined total of 28), taking care to conserve as much of the remainder of the print as possible. From these 28 rectangles, cut a *combined* total of 36 squares, 1½″ × 1½″.

Reserve the remainder of the 28 assorted prints.

From the remainder of the 28 assorted prints, choose your 7 favorite prints; from *each* of these prints, cut:

1 binding strip, 2½″ × the length of the fabric, for a combined total of 7 binding strips (for my chubby binding method provided on page 126, reduce the strip width to 2″)

Reserve the scraps of these assorted prints.

From the remainder of all 28 assorted prints, cut:

Length-of-fabric strips in a variety of widths ranging from ¾″ to 1¼″. (Please note that the number of strips needed will vary depending upon the strip widths chosen, so I suggest cutting as many strips as possible using all of the remaining assorted prints.)

From *each* of the 5 assorted cream prints, cut:

1 rectangle, 1½″ × 9″, from one short end of the print (total of 5). Crosscut into 5 squares, 1½″ × 1½″ (*combined* total of 25 squares).

Reserve the remainder of the cream prints.

From the remainder of the cream prints, choose your 3 favorite prints; from *each* of these 3 prints, cut:

1 additional rectangle, 1½″ × 9″, from one short end of the print. From these rectangles, cut a *combined* total of 11 squares, 1½″ × 1½″ (grand total of 36 with previously cut squares).

Reserve the scraps of these 3 cream prints.

From the remainder of all 5 cream prints, cut a *combined* total of:

12 strips, 2⅞″ × length of fabric

PIECING THE STRING BLOCKS

Sew all pieces with right sides together using a ¼″ seam allowance unless otherwise noted. Press the seam allowances as indicated by the arrows or otherwise specified.

1. Using a slightly scant seam allowance (two or three threads less than ¼″) and choosing the assorted prints randomly, join a variety of strips widths along the long edges to make a pieced strip approximately 2¾″ to 3″ wide. Press. Repeat to stitch 18 pieced strips approximately 19½″ long.

Make 18 pieced strips, 2¾″–3″ wide and approximately 19½″ long.

2. Join a cream 2⅞″-wide strip to one long edge of a pieced strip from step 1. Press. Repeat to piece a total of 12 strip-set strips measuring approximately 18″ to 19½″ in length. Reserve the remaining pieced strips for use in the border.

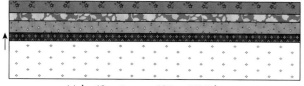

Make 12 strip sets, 18″ to 19½″ long.

3. Use a square acrylic ruler (a 6″ × 6″ size works well for me) and a rotary cutter to cut a total of 36 patchwork squares, 3½″ × 3½″, from the strip sets making sure the center diagonal of each square runs through the seamline of the cream strip. Reserve any unused strip-set ends for use in the border, if needed.

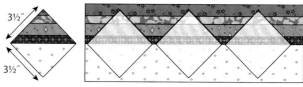

3½″

3½″

Cut 36 patchwork squares, 3½″ × 3½″.

4. Use a pencil and an acrylic ruler to draw a diagonal sewing line from corner to corner on the wrong side of the 36 cream and 36 assorted-print 1½″ squares.

5. Layer a prepared cream square and a prepared print 1½″ square onto two opposite corners of a step 3 patchwork square as shown. Stitch the small squares along the drawn lines. Fold the resulting inner triangles open, aligning the corners with the corners of the larger square underneath. Press. Trim away the layers beneath the top triangles, leaving ¼″ seam

Traffic Jam

Finished quilt size: 22½″ × 22½″ ✦ **Finished block size: 6″ × 6″**

Designed and pieced by Kim Diehl. Machine quilted by Connie Tabor.

allowances. Repeat to piece a total of 36 String block quadrants measuring 3½″ square, including the seam allowances.

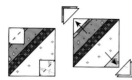

Make 36 quarter-block units, 3½″ × 3½″.

6. Lay out four block quadrants in two horizontal rows as shown. Join the units in each row. Press. Join the rows. Press. Repeat to piece a total of nine String blocks measuring 6½″ square, including the seam allowances.

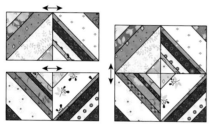

Make 9 blocks, 6½″ × 6½″.

PIECING THE QUILT CENTER

Lay out nine String blocks in three horizontal rows of three blocks. Join the blocks. Press. Join the rows. Press. The pieced quilt center should measure 18½″ square, including the seam allowances.

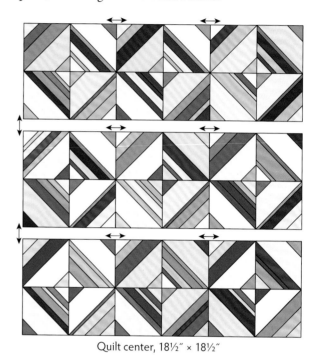

Quilt center, 18½″ × 18½″

PIECING AND ADDING THE BORDER

1. Using the reserved strip sets and any useable scraps from the previously used strip-set ends, cut a total of 40 pieced squares, 2½″ × 2½″. (Note: For more variation in the prints used in my patchwork, I cut my 2½″ squares from alternating sides of the strip set as shown.)

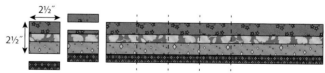

Cut 40 pieced squares, 2½″ × 2½″.

2. Lay out nine pieced squares end to end as shown, rotating every other square a quarter turn to form the design. Join the squares. Press. Repeat to piece two border strips. Join these pieced strips to the right and left sides of the quilt center. Press. In the same manner, refer use the remaining pieced squares to stitch two additional border strips consisting of 11 squares each, starting and ending with the strips facing horizontally. The border strips should measure 22½″ long. Join these pieced strips to the top and bottom edges of the quilt center. Press.

Quilt assembly

COMPLETING THE QUILT

Layer and baste the quilt top, batting, and backing. Quilt the layers. The featured quilt is machine quilted with an edge-to-edge design of serpentine feathered vines. Cut the binding strips into smaller random lengths as desired, and then join them to make a pieced binding strip; use this strip to bind the quilt.

Bricks and Mortar

Scrappy quilts such as this present an incredibly fun opportunity to raid your scrap basket and throw traditional color guidelines out the window. Embrace your creativity as you experiment with unique and unusual print pairings, and be pleasantly surprised by the outcome as you build your quilt rows brick by brick.

MATERIALS

Yardage is based on a 42″ width of useable fabric after prewashing and removing selvages.

- Approximately ⅔ yard *total* of scraps that are at least 3″ × 3″ for blocks
- 1 fat quarter (18″ × 21″) of dark print for the border, and optional use in the blocks
- 1 fat quarter of complimentary print for the binding, and optional use in the blocks
- 1 fat quarter of print for backing
- 18″ × 21″ piece of batting

DESIGN NOTES

Because of the scrappy style of this quilt design, and a block layout that lets *you* choose the combinations of colors and how often they're used, I found it was best to begin by cutting a variety of 3″ squares (which are then cut in half diagonally twice to form triangles) for the bulk of the hourglass units that make up the needed bricks. This approach will give you a nice pile of pre-cut triangles to draw from as you stitch the patchwork, without a lot of needed starts and stops to cut more triangles while you work. As your design takes shape, it's easy to occasionally fill in here and there with additional triangles.

Keeping in mind that one square will yield four triangles in a single matching print, I began with approximately 70 squares from assorted prints. If it was a print I really loved and thought I might use for three or more hourglass units, I cut two squares and kept the resulting triangles grouped together by print.

For prints that I liked but wasn't sure I'd use for more than one or two hourglass units, I began with one square. This is a great jumping-off point to begin the project, making it easy to adapt, divide, and conquer as you assemble your rows.

Please refer to the quilt assembly diagram on page 76 to see how I divided my hourglass units into bricks, and how I mingled a small sprinkling of cream prints into the design for a bit of sparkle. Or, create your own layout!

CUTTING

Cut all pieces across the width of the fabric in the order given unless otherwise noted.

From the print chosen for the border, cut:
4 strips, 2″ × 21″; crosscut into 4 strips, 2″ × 15½″

From the print chosen for the binding, cut:
4 binding strips, 2½″ × 21″. (For Kim's chubby binding method provided on page 126, reduce the strip width to 2″.)

From assorted-print scraps, including the remainders the border and binding (if desired), cut:
Approximately 70 squares, 3″ × 3″, in a variety of complimentary colors. (Cut 2 squares from prints you might want to use more often.) Cut each square in half diagonally *twice* to yield 4 triangles. Keep the triangles organized by print.

PIECING THE HOURGLASS UNITS

Sew all pieces with right sides together using a ¼″ seam allowance unless otherwise noted. Press the seam allowances as indicated by the arrows or otherwise specified.

1. To piece one hourglass unit, select two matching-print triangles *each* from two complimentary prints. Reserve the remaining triangles from these prints and draw from them as you wish to piece the remaining hourglass units.

2. Lay out the four triangles in two diagonal rows as shown. Join the triangles in each row. Press. Join the rows. Use a rotary cutter and a small square acrylic ruler featuring a center diagonal line to trim the pieced unit to a measurement of 2″ square, removing the dog-ear points in the same step.

3. Referring to the assembly diagram at right for the general number of units to stitch in each color pairing, continue piecing the hourglass units. Keep the hourglass units organized by print. You'll need 80 hourglass units, but you may want to piece more for layout options.

PIECING THE BRICK ROWS AND ASSEMBLING THE QUILT CENTER

1. Lay out eight hourglass units for row 1, referring to the assembly diagram for the color placement guidance. Join the units. Press all seam allowances to one side.

2. Continue laying out, joining, and pressing the units to build the remaining brick rows. For added interest, I chose to occasionally give an hourglass unit a quarter turn for an unexpected design element—this is entirely up to you! As you work through the rows you may need to piece a handful of additional hourglass units to complete your design, and, depending upon your color choices, you may have some leftover triangles.

3. Join the rows to complete the quilt center. Press the seam allowances open. The pieced quilt center should measure 12½″ × 15½″, including the seam allowances.

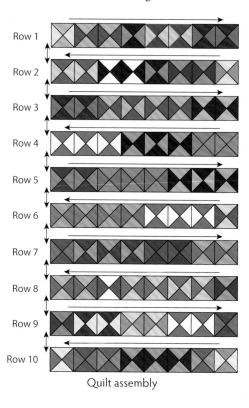

Quilt assembly

ADDING THE BORDER

Join a 2″ × 15½″ border strip to the right and left sides of the quilt center. Press the seam allowances toward the border strips. Join the remaining 2″ × 15½″ border strips to the top and bottom edges of the quilt center. Press the seam allowances toward the newly added border strips.

COMPLETING THE QUILT

Layer and baste the quilt top, batting, and backing. Quilt the layers. The featured quilt is machine quilted with an edge-to-edge repeating orange-peel design. Join the binding strips to make one length and use it to bind the quilt.

Bricks and Mortar

FINISHED QUILT SIZE: 15½″ × 18½″

Designed and pieced by Kim Diehl. Machine quilted by Connie Tabor.

Piece and Plenty

Overflowing with pieced pinwheels and a plentiful sprinkling of scraps, this patchwork mini is the ultimate scrap buster. Dive into your stash, rescue even the smallest bits of your favorite saved prints, and repurpose them into this fun-to-stitch project.

MATERIALS

Yardage is based on a 42″ width of useable fabric after prewashing and removing selvages. Please note that yardage amounts for the cream and assorted prints are approximate guidelines only, as the rectangle and square sizes you choose to cut when stitching the border will affect the amount of fabric used.

- Approximately 1 yard *total* of assorted-print scraps (collectively referred to as "dark"), in 3″ square sizes and smaller, for blocks, setting squares, and border
- Approximately ⅓ yard *total* of assorted cream scraps, in 3″ square sizes and smaller, for blocks and setting squares
- 1 fat quarter (18″ × 21″) of complimentary print for the binding
- ¾ yard of fabric for backing
- 27″ × 27″ square of batting

CUTTING

This quilt features a free-style border, meaning that scraps in a variety of widths can be used for the rectangles and squares to accommodate your stash; once the border units have been pieced they can be trimmed to the needed size. With this in mind, the quantities provided at right will give you a good number of pieces to start with. More pieces can be added as needed, and any leftover pieces that remain after the border piecing steps can be placed back into your stash.

From the dark scraps, cut a *total* of:

100 rectangles, 1¾″ × 3″; keep the rectangles organized into a pinwheel patchwork set.

12 squares, 3″ × 3″; keep the squares organized into a setting block set.

100 rectangles, 3″ long by 1¼″, 1½″, and 1″ wide (I cut most scraps 1¼″ wide, but some at 1½″ and 1″.) Keep rectangles organized in a piano-key border set.

Approximately 40 squares, 1½″ × 1½″

Approximately 40 squares, 1¼″ × 1¼″; keep the squares organized by size into two checkerboard border sets.

From assorted cream scraps, for the Pinwheel Variation blocks, cut a *total* of:

50 squares, 3″ × 3″; cut each square in half diagonally *once* to yield 2 triangles (combined total of 100). Keep the cream triangles organized into a cream pinwheel patchwork set.

From assorted cream scraps, for the setting squares, cut a *total* of:

12 squares, 3″ × 3″

From the binding fabric, cut:

5 strips, 2½″ × 21″ (For my chubby binding method on page 126, reduce the strip width to 2″.)

Piecing the Pinwheel Variation Blocks

Sew all pieces with right sides together using a ¼″ seam allowance unless otherwise noted. Press the seam allowances as indicated by the arrows or otherwise specified.

1. Select the pinwheel patchwork set. Choose two 1¾″ × 3″ rectangles in complimentary colors. Join the rectangles along the long edges. Press. Repeat to sew a total of 50 pieced squares measuring 3″ square, including the seam allowances.

Make 50 pieced sqares, 3″ × 3″.

2. Use a rotary cutter and an acrylic ruler to cut each pieced rectangle in half diagonally *once* to yield two pieced triangles (total of 100).

Cut pieced squares in half diagonally.

3. Using the cream pinwheel patchwork set, join a cream triangle to a pieced triangle from step 2. Press. Repeat to sew a total of 100 pieced half-square-triangle units measuring approximately 2½″ square.

Make 100 pieced triangle units, 2½″ × 2½″.

4. Using a rotary cutter and a small acrylic ruler featuring a center diagonal line, measure out from the dark triangle corner to trim away the excess fabric on two sides of the block so it measures 1⅞″ square. (The dog-ear points will be removed in this step). Rotate the unit and trim *only* the dog-ear points from the remaining corner of the unit, squaring up the sides in the same step, and keeping the measurement at 1⅞″ square. Repeat to trim all 100 units.

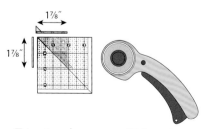

Trim pieced squares to 1⅞″ square.

FINISHED QUILT SIZE: 22½″ × 22½″ ◆ FINISHED BLOCK SIZE: 2½″ × 2½″

Designed and pieced by Kim Diehl. Machine quilted by Connie Tabor.

5. Choose four trimmed half-square-triangle units and lay them out in two horizontal rows to form a pinwheel design. Join the units in each row. Press. Join the rows. Press. Use a rotary cutter and an acrylic ruler to trim the Pinwheel Variation block to measure 3″ square. Repeat to piece a total of 25 Pinwheel Variation blocks. For added interest, I made approximately half of my blocks with the dark paddle pieces positioned in a mirror image from the original blocks—this is entirely up to you!

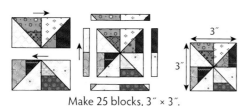

Make 25 blocks, 3″ × 3″.

PIECING THE QUILT CENTER

Lay out the 25 Pinwheel Variation blocks, the 12 dark 3″ setting squares, and the 12 cream 3″ setting squares in seven horizontal rows as shown in the quilt assembly diagram. If you chose to include mirror-image Pinwheel variation blocks for added interest, position them randomly. Join the pieces in each row. Press. The pieced quilt center should measure 18″ square, including the seam allowances.

Quilt assembly

PIECING AND ADDING THE FREE-STYLE PIANO KEY BORDER

The free-style piano key border in this quilt is meant to come together in a fluid way, letting you choose the size of your rectangles and squares, and laying out the design in a way that pleases you. I used four or five pieced checkerboard rectangles for each side of my border; you can follow this guideline, or create a layout with your own preferred amount of checkerboard.

1. Select the checkerboard border patchwork set. Choose three to four squares of the same size (either 1½″ or 1¼″ square), in complimentary colors. Join the squares. Press. Repeat, using squares of the same size for each unit, to make approximately 20 pieced checkerboard rectangles measuring 3″ or longer.

Make approximately 20 units, 3″ or longer.

2. Using the dark 3″-long rectangles in varying widths, lay out enough rectangles and checkerboard units to form a free-style piano key border strip measuring slightly longer than 18″. Join the rectangles. Press. Repeat to piece a total of four border strips measuring a bit longer than 18″ in length. Use a rotary cutter and an acrylic ruler to trim away any excess fabric from the checkerboard rectangles to keep the long side edges flush.

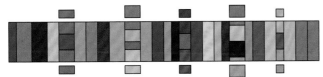

Make 4 border strips, 3″ × more than 18″.

3. Centering each strip along the edge of the quilt, join a border strip to the right and left sides of the quilt center. Press the seam allowances toward the border strips. Use a rotary cutter and an acrylic ruler to trim away any excess border length from each end of the strips.

4. Join additional rectangles and/or pieced checkerboard rectangles to the two remaining border strips from step 2 to bring the length to approximately 24″. Press. Join, press, and trim these two completed border strips to the top and bottom edges of the quilt center, so the pieced quilt top measures 22½″ square, including the seam allowances.

COMPLETING THE QUILT

Layer and baste the quilt top, batting, and backing. Quilt the layers. The featured quilt is machine quilted with an edge-to-edge scalloped clamshell design. Join the complimentary-print binding strips to make one length and use it to bind the quilt.

Hayride

With very simply sewn patchwork that comes together in a jiffy, this mini quilt features small blocks that blend together so seamlessly, it's hard to tell where one begins and the other ends. Glance once and you may see chocolate-hued pinwheels; look again, and your eyes might be drawn to spinning stars. Can you spot the block?

MATERIALS

Yardages are based on a 42″ width of useable fabric after prewashing and removing selvages.

- 2 fat eighths (9″ × 21″) of brown prints for patchwork
- 5 fat eighths of assorted cream prints for patchwork
- 22 charm squares (5″ × 5″) of assorted prints for patchwork
- 1 fat quarter (18″ × 21″) of black print for patchwork and binding
- ⅔ yard of fabric for backing
- 23″ × 23″ square of batting

CUTTING

Cut all pieces across the width of the fabric in the order given unless otherwise noted.

From *each* of the 2 brown prints, cut:
4 strips, 1½″ × 21″ (combined total of 8); crosscut into 32 rectangles, 1½″ × 2½″ (combined total of 64)
Keep the pieces organized by print into 2 brown patchwork sets.

From *each* of the 5 assorted cream prints, cut:
3 strips, 1½″ × 21″ (combined total of 15); crosscut into 39 squares, 1½″ × 1½″ (combined total of 195)

From *each* of the assorted-print charm squares, cut:
3 rectangles, 1½″ × 2½″ (combined total of 66)

From the black print, cut:
1 strip, 1½″ × 21″; crosscut into 3 rectangles, 1½″ × 2½″ (grand total of 69, with previously cut assorted-print rectangles)
4 binding strips, 2½″ × 21″ (for my chubby binding method provided on page 126, reduce the strip width to 2″)

PIECING THE WHIRLIGIG BLOCKS

Sew all pieces with right sides together using a ¼″ seam allowance unless otherwise noted. Press the seam allowances as indicated by the arrows or otherwise specified.

1. For the Whirligig A blocks, select one of the brown patchwork sets and 32 assorted-print 1½″ × 2½″ rectangles (including some cut from the black print), and 96 cream 1½″ squares. Use a pencil and an acrylic ruler to draw a diagonal sewing line from corner to corner on the wrong side of each cream square.

2. Layer a prepared cream square onto one end of a brown rectangle as shown. Stitch the pair together along the drawn line. Fold the resulting inner cream triangle open, aligning the corner with the corner of the brown rectangle. Press. Trim away the layers beneath the top triangle, leaving a ¼″ seam allowance. In the same manner, add a second cream triangle to the remaining end of the brown rectangle. Repeat to piece a total of 32 double-triangle patchwork units measuring 1½″ × 2½″, including the seam allowances.

Make 12 units, 1½″ × 2½″.

3. Using the remaining prepared cream 1½" squares and the assorted-print 1½" × 2½" rectangles selected in step 1, refer to step 2 to piece a total of 32 single-triangle patchwork units measuring 1½" × 2½".

Make 32 units, 1½" × 2½".

4. Join a single-triangle patchwork unit to the top edge of a double-triangle patchwork unit. Press. Repeat to piece a total of 32 block quadrants measuring 2½" × 2½", including the seam allowances.

Make 32 block quadrants, 2½" × 2½".

5. Lay out four quadrants in two horizontal rows, rotating the units as shown. Join the units in each row. Press. Join the rows. Press. Repeat to piece a total of eight Whirligig A blocks measuring 4½" square, including the seam allowances.

Make 9 Whirligig A blocks, 4½" × 4½".

6. Using the second brown patchwork set, the remaining 1½" cream squares, and the assorted-print 1½" × 2½" rectangles, repeat steps 1–5 to piece a total of eight Whirligig B blocks measuring 4½" square, including the seam allowances. (Please note that you'll have a small handful of leftover assorted-print rectangles and cream squares; these have been included for added choices as you stitch the patchwork.)

Make 8 Whirligig B blocks, 4½" × 4½".

PIECING THE QUILT TOP

1. Lay out two Whirligig A blocks and two Whirligig B blocks in alternating positions as shown. Join the blocks. Repeat to piece a total of two A rows measuring 4½" × 16½", including the seam allowances.

Make 2 A rows, 4½" × 16½".

2. Lay out two Whirligig B blocks and two Whirligig A blocks in alternating positions as shown. Join the blocks. Press. Repeat to piece a total of two B rows measuring 4½" × 16½", including the seam allowances.

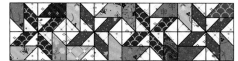

Make 2 B rows, 4½" × 16½".

3. Referring to the quilt assembly diagram, lay out the A and B rows in alternating positions. Join the rows. Press the seam allowances of each row to one side, in the direction that produces the best points.

Quilt assembly

COMPLETING THE QUILT

Layer and baste the quilt top, batting, and backing. Quilt the layers. The featured quilt was machine quilted with an edge-to-edge design of swirls made from clusters of echoed serpentine lines. Join the black binding strips to make one length and use it to bind the quilt.

Hayride

FINISHED QUILT SIZE: 16½" × 16½" ◆ FINISHED BLOCK SIZE: 4½" × 4½"

Designed and pieced by Kim Diehl. Machine quilted by Connie Tabor.

Pleased as Punch

Sew sparkling stars and surround them with strippy patchwork, stitch "almost stars" into colorful Lily blocks, and then piece Nine Patches into alluring bits of checkerboard. Mingle them together and what do you get? One pleasing patchwork project, briming over with tradition and charm.

MATERIALS

Yardage is based on a 42" width of useable fabric after prewashing and removing selvages.

+ 8 fat eighths (9" × 21") of assorted cream prints for blocks
+ 20 chubby sixteenths (9" × 10½") of assorted prints for blocks, border, and binding
+ ½ yard of black print for blocks and border
+ 1 yard of fabric for backing
+ 36" × 36" square of batting

CUTTING

Cut all pieces across the width of the fabric in the order given unless otherwise noted. WOF is defined as width of fabric.

From *each* of the 8 cream prints, cut:

2 strips, 1½" × 21" (combined total of 16); crosscut into:
  10 rectangles, 1½" × 2½" (combined total of 80)
  8 squares, 1½" × 1½" (combined total of 64)
Organize the above pieces into a cream Lily block patchwork set.

2 strips, 1½" × 21" (combined total of 16); crosscut into:
  2 rectangles, 1½" × 2½" (combined total of 16)
  2 rectangles, 1½" × 4½" (combined total of 16)
  2 rectangles, 1½" × 6½" (combined total of 16)
Organize the above pieces into a cream Star block patchwork set.

From *each* of the 20 assorted prints, cut:

1 binding strip, 2½" × 10" (combined total of 20). (For my chubby binding method on page 126, reduce the strip width to 2".)
2 strips, 1½" × 10½"; crosscut into:
  7 squares, 1½" × 1½" (combined total of 140)
  1 rectangle, 1½" × 2½" (combined total of 20)
Group the above squares and rectangles by print into an assorted-print Lily block patchwork sets. Reserve the remainder of the 20 assorted prints.

From the remainder of *each of 8 assorted prints*, cut:

1 strip, 1½" × 10½" (combined total of 8); crosscut into
  4 squares, 1½" × 1½" (combined total of 32).
Group the above squares by print and organize them into a Nine Patch A patchwork set.

From the remainder of *each of 4 assorted prints*, cut:

1 strip, 1½" × 10½" (combined total of 4); crosscut into
  5 squares, 1½" × 1½" (combined total of 20).
Group the above squares by print and organize them into a Nine Patch B patchwork set.]

From the reserved scraps of *all* assorted prints, cut a *combined* total of:

48 squares, 1½" × 1½"
Organize the above squares into an assorted-print Star block patchwork set.

From the black print, cut:

1 strip, 2½" × WOF; from this strip, cut 4 squares, 2½" × 2½", and 20 squares, 1½" × 1½"
4 strips, 1½" × WOF; crosscut into 108 squares, 1½" × 1½" (total of 128 with previously cut squares)
2 strips, 3½" × WOF; crosscut into 4 strips, 3½" × 18½"

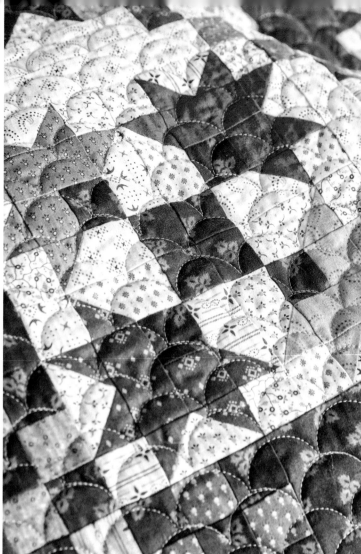

PIECING THE LILY BLOCKS

Sew all pieces with right sides together using a ¼″ seam allowance unless otherwise noted. Press the seam allowances as indicated by the arrows other otherwise specified.

1. Select the assorted-print and cream Lily block patchwork sets. Use a pencil and an acrylic ruler to draw a diagonal sewing line from corner to corner on the wrong side of six of the seven 1½″ squares cut from each assorted print, continuing to keep all pieces grouped by print.

2. Choose one set of grouped pieces consisting of six prepared 1½″ squares from a single print, one matching-print 1½″ square, and one matching-print 1½″ × 2½″ rectangle (referred to as "dark" from this point forward). From the cream Lily block patchwork set, choose four assorted cream 1½″ × 2½″ rectangles, and three assorted cream 1½″ squares.

3. Layer a prepared dark 1½″ square onto one end of an assorted cream 1½″ × 2½″ rectangle. Stitch the square along the drawn diagonal line. Fold the resulting inner dark triangle open, aligning the corner with the corner of the rectangle. Press. Trim away the layers beneath the top triangle, leaving a ¼″ seam allowance. In the same manner, add a mirror-image triangle to the remaining end of the rectangle. Repeat to piece a total of two flying-geese units measuring 1½″ × 2½″, including the seam allowances.

Make 2 flying geese units, 1½″ × 2½″.

4. Using the two remaining prepared dark 1½″ squares, follow step 3 to piece one single-star-point unit and one mirror-image single-star-point unit measuring 1½″ × 2½″, including the seam allowances.

Make 1 unit and 1 mirror-imgae unit, 1½″ × 2½″.

FINISHED QUILT SIZE: 30½″ × 30½″ • FINISHED BLOCK SIZE: 8½″ × 8½″

Designed by Kim Diehl. Pieced by Jennifer Martinez. Machine quilted by Connie Tabor.

5. Lay out the unmarked dark 1½˝ square, the matching dark 1½˝ × 2½˝ rectangle, and one black 1½˝ square in two horizontal rows as shown. Join the squares in the bottom row. Press. Join the rows. Press. The pieced center square unit should measure 2½˝ square, including the seam allowances.

Make 1 center square unit, 2½˝ × 2½˝.

6. Lay out the center square unit, the two flying-geese units from step 3, the two single-star-point units from step 4, three cream 1½˝ squares, and one black 1½˝ square in three horizontal rows as shown. Join the pieces in each row. Press. Join the rows. Press. The pieced lily unit should measure 4½˝ square, including the seam allowances.

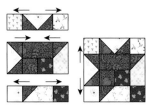

Lily unit, 4½˝ × 4½˝

7. Repeat steps 2–6 to piece a total of 20 lily units. Please note that you'll have a handful of unused cream 1½˝ squares. Reserve the remaining black 1½˝ squares for later use.

8. Lay out four lily units in two horizontal rows, rotating the units as shown. Join the units in each row. Press. Join the rows. Press. Repeat to piece a total of five Lily blocks measuring 8½˝ square, including the seam allowances.

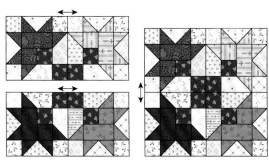

Make 5 Lily blocks, 8½˝ × 8½˝.

PIECING THE STAR BLOCKS

1. Use a pencil and an acrylic ruler to prepare 32 black 1½˝ squares with a diagonal sewing line as previously instructed.

2. Select eight prepared black squares, and one black 2½˝ square. From the cream Star block patchwork set, choose four rectangles *each* in 2½˝, 4½˝, and 6½˝ lengths. Last, from the assorted-print Star block patchwork set, randomly choose 12 squares, 1½˝ × 1½˝.

3. Use the four cream 2½˝-long rectangles and the eight prepared black 1½˝ squares to piece four black star-point units, 1½˝ × 2½˝, as previously instructed.

Make 4 black units, 1½˝ × 2½˝.

4. Lay out the four black star-point units, the black 2½˝ square, and four dark 1½˝ squares in three horizontal rows as shown. Join the pieces in each row. Press. Join the rows. Press. The pieced center star unit should measure 4½˝ square, including the seam allowances.

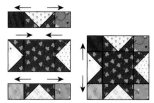

Center star unit, 4½˝ × 4½˝

5. Join a cream 1½˝ × 4½˝ rectangle to the right and left sides of the center star unit. Press. Sew an dark 1½˝ square to each end of the remaining two cream 4½˝-long rectangles. Press. Join these pieced cream rectangles to the top and bottom edges of the center star unit. The pieced star unit should now measure 6½˝ square, including the seam allowances.

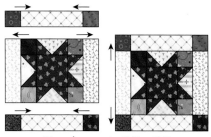

Pieced star unit, 6½˝ × 6½˝

6. Using four cream 1½″ × 6½″ rectangles and four assorted dark 1½″ squares, repeat step 5 to complete the Star block and bring the measurement to 8½″ square, including the seam allowances.

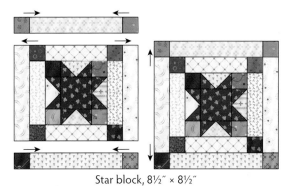

Star block, 8½″ × 8½″

7. Repeat steps 2–6 to piece a total of four Star blocks.

PIECING THE QUILT CENTER

Lay out the five pieced Lily blocks and the four pieced Star blocks in three horizontal rows, alternating the blocks as shown. Join the blocks in each row. Press. Join the rows. Press. The pieced quilt center should measure 24½″ square, including the seam allowances.

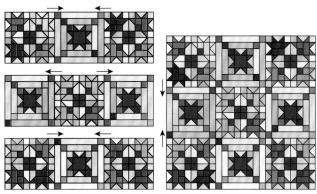

Quilt center, 24½″ × 24½″

PIECING AND ADDING THE BORDER

1. Select the Nine-Patch A patchwork set and choose four squares cut from a single matching print. Lay out the four squares with five black 1½″ squares in three horizontal rows as shown. Join the squares in each row. Press. Join the rows. Press. Repeat to piece a total of eight Nine Patch A blocks measuring 3½″ square, including the seam allowances.

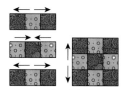

Make 8 Nine Patch A blocks, 3½″ × 3½″.

2. Select the Nine-Patch B patchwork set. Using five squares cut from a single matching print and four black 1½″ squares, repeat step 1 to piece a total of four Nine Patch B blocks measuring 3½″ square, including the seam allowances.

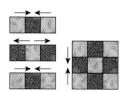

3. Referring to the quilt assembly diagram, join a Nine Patch A block from step 1 to each end of a black 3½″ × 18½″ strip. Press. Join these pieced strips to the right and left sides of the quilt center. Press. Again referring to the illustration, join Nine Patch A and B blocks to each end of the remaining black 3½″ × 18½″ strips. Press. Join these pieced strips to the remaining sides of the quilt center. Press.

Quilt assembly

Easy (and Cute) Binding Storage

My favorite repurposed item for organizing bindings in my sewing room is a string holder. These holders can be found in the home dec, crafting, or office section of many stores and are available in a variety of sizes and styles to suit your decor. They often come with string or twine already wrapped around the center rod, which is a good thing! To make the holder functional for holding my binding with minimal "slippage," I remove most of the string, leaving a few layers intact. After cutting and preparing my binding, I anchor one end to the string using a straight pin, wrap it securely in place around the center rod, and secure the outer end with an additional pin. Anchoring the binding in this way enables me to store three or four bindings at a time, and keeps them in pristine condition until I'm ready to use them. As an added bonus, my little holder looks really pretty sitting on the shelf!

COMPLETING THE QUILT

Layer and baste the quilt top, batting, and backing. Quilt the layers. The featured quilt is machine quilted with an edge-to-edge clamshell design. Cut the assorted-print 2½″ × 10½″ binding strips into smaller random lengths if desired, join them together to make one scrappy length, and use it to bind the quilt.

Autumn Acorn Mug Mat

What could be better than sipping a steaming mug of something warm and tasty on a crisp and cool day? Having a "sip and sit" with a mug mat that blends autumn with nearly every quilter's favorite thing—a sparkling star! Gift one of these mug mats to a friend, tuck my recipe for gingerbread syrup (see page 101) into a mug, and you'll make someone feel very special.

MATERIALS

Yardage is based on a 42" width of useable fabric after prewashing and removing selvages.

+ 1 square, 10½" × 10½", of cream print for star background and backing

+ 1 square, 2" × 2", of gold print for star center square

+ 1 charm square (5" × 5") *each* of dark green, cranberry, and orange prints for star patchwork

+ 1 rectangle, 3" × 6", of brown print for acorn cap

+ 1 rectangle, 1¾" × 5", of medium green pint for acorn stem

+ 1 sheet, 8½" × 11", of freezer paper to make pattern pieces

+ 1 rectangle, 5½" × 6½", of batting for mug mat filler

+ Size 5 embroidery needle for big-stitch hand-quilting accents

+ #12 Valdani perle cotton in color O-501, variegated ebony and almond, for big-stitch hand-quilting accents

CUTTING

Cut all pieces across the width of the fabric in the order given unless otherwise noted.

From the cream print, cut:
2 strips, 2" × 10½"; crosscut into 8 squares, 2" × 2"
Reserve the remainder of the tan print for the mug mat backing.

From *each* of the dark green, cranberry, and orange prints, cut:
4 squares, 1¼" × 1¼" (combined total of 12)
Keep the squares organized by print.

PIECING THE STAR UNIT

Sew all pieces with right sides together using a ¼″ seam allowance unless otherwise noted. Press the seam allowances as indicated by the arrows, or otherwise instructed.

1. Use a pencil and an acrylic ruler to draw a diagonal sewing line from corner to corner on the wrong side of each dark green, cranberry, and orange square.

2. Referring to the illustration, layer a prepared green square onto two opposite corners of the gold 2″ square. Stitch the green squares along the drawn diagonal lines, just *next* to each line on the side closest to the outer corner (this will compensate for the tiny bit of fabric lost to the fold when the stitched triangle point is pressed open). Fold each resulting green triangle open, aligning the corner with the corner of the square. Press. Trim away the layers beneath the top triangle, leaving ¼″ seam allowances. In the same manner, add stitched green triangles to the remaining corners of the gold square. The pieced square-in-a-square unit should measure 2″ square, including the seam allowances.

Make 1 unit, 2″ × 2″.

3. Using four tan 2″ squares and the prepared cranberry and orange squares from step 1, follow step 2 to add a cranberry triangle to the bottom right and an orange triangle to the bottom left of each tan square. Repeat to make a total of four pieced star-point units measuring 2″ square, taking care to position the cranberry and orange squares identically in each unit.

Make 4 units, 2″ × 2″.

4. Lay out the four star-point units from step 3, the square-in-a-square unit from step 2, and the four remaining tan 2″ squares in three horizontal rows as shown. Join the pieces in each row. Press the seam allowances of the top and bottom rows toward the corner tan squares. Press the seam allowances of the middle row toward the center square-in-a-square unit. Join the rows. Press the seam allowances away toward the top and bottom rows. The pieced star unit should measure 5″ square, including the seam allowances.

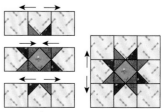

Make 1 star unit, 5″ × 5″.

Finished mug mat size: approximately 4½″ × 5¼″, excluding stem

Designed, pieced, machine quilted, and hand quilted by Kim Diehl.

MAKING THE MUG MAT FRONT

1. Trace the acorn cap and acorn bottom from the patterns on page 103 onto the dull side of a piece of freezer paper, making sure to include the dashed lines showing the ¼″ seam allowances at the top and bottom edges. Cut out the pattern pieces exactly along each traced outer solid shape outline. (The seam allowances have been built into the remainder of the shapes, so there's no need to add more.)

2. Position the cut acorn bottom shape onto the pieced star unit, centering it from right to left and positioning the top straight edge so it rests ¼″ above the topmost star points. Beginning with the top edge, use a pencil to trace the shape onto the star block. Because of individual seam allowance variations that can occur when piecing the star, if the bottom star points appear that they may land within the ¼″ seam allowance therefore cutting off the tips, after tracing the top of the shape, slide the pattern downward a few threads before finishing the tracing. Use a rotary cutter and an acrylic ruler to cut away the top portion of the star unit, a thread or two above the traced top line of the acorn.

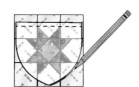

Trace acorn shape onto star unit and cut away top of unit along drawn line.

3. Position the trimmed unit onto the brown 3″ × 6″ acorn-cap rectangle, right sides together and centering the star from right to left and aligning the top edges. Pin the top edges in place. Stitch the top pinned edges using a ¼″ seam allowance. Remove the pins, flip the brown rectangle open, and press the seam allowances toward the brown print.

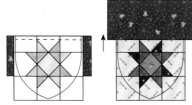

Attach brown rectangle to top of star unit.

4. Position the acorn cap freezer-paper pattern onto the front unit, aligning the sides of the pattern piece with the drawn straight side edges of the acorn bottom. The curves begin at the bottom edge of the brown print. Use a pencil or a fine-tipped marker to trace the acorn cap shape onto the brown print.

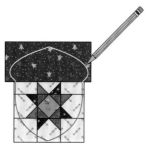

Trace acorn cap onto top rectangle.

5. Layer the prepared front unit onto the rectangle of batting; use straight pins to anchor the layers to prevent shifting. (There's no need to add a backing piece yet.) Referring to the mug mat pictured on page 99, use your sewing machine and brown or neutral thread to machine quilt the top brown portion of the unit as desired. (I stitched straight horizontal lines beginning ⅜″ from the pieced bottom brown edge, repeating them at even intervals until I reached the top of the unit. Next, I stitched diagonal lines at approximately a 60° angle to create an elongated crosshatch; just estimate this and have fun as you stitch!

6. With the medium green 1¾″ × 5″ rectangle wrong side down, fold the long raw edges to the center (you should now be seeing the "pretty" side of the print) so they meet in the middle and press them in place with a hot iron. Next, fold the rectangle in half lengthwise to encase the long raw edges. Machine stitch the folded long edges together, approximately three or four threads in from the edge, to complete the stem.

Stitch along the open long edge to secure.

7. Fold the stitched stem in half, aligning the raw ends and offsetting them very slightly to form a small loop. Position the raw ends of the folded stem onto the front of the acorn unit, centering them at the point of the acorn cap, with the bottom loop approximately ¼″–½″ from the bottom brown edge; pin in place. You can shorten the stem by positioning the looped end further up from the bottom brown edge, so please yourself! Any excess stem length extending beyond the top edge of the unit will be trimmed away later.

Pin raw edges of stem in place.

8. Use a size 5 embroidery needle and #12 perle cotton to add big-stitch hand-quilting accents to the star portion of the front unit as desired. (I outlined the gold square in the square-in-a-square center, and then outlined the star just outside the seam lines.)

9. Machine stitch in the seam of each star-point on the right side of the front unit, a few threads inside the drawn line of the acorn shape, to help the seams stay intact as they're handled in the final steps. In the same manner, stitch the pinned top edges of the stem a few threads inside the drawn line of the acorn cap shape to anchor it to the front. Trim away any excess stem length that extends above the top of the unit.

COMPLETING THE MUG MAT

1. Position the mug mat front onto the backing piece, with the backing print right side up. Pin the layers around the acorn edges to secure them, positioning the pins inside the acorn shape as shown to prevent shifting and out of the way of your scissors. Use sharp scissors to cut out the acorn exactly along the drawn shape line, remembering that the seam allowance has already been included so there's no need to add more.

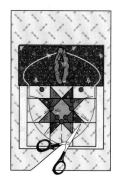

Trim acorn front and backing, cutting along marked lines.

2. Remove the pins and place the backing *wrong side up* onto the front of the acorn, (the "pretty" sides of the prints will now be facing one another, you'll be looking at the wrong side of the backing piece), centering it to fit exactly. Pin the layers securely along the acorn edges.

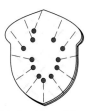

Pin acorn front to backing, right sides together.

3. Beginning at the bottom right star-point edge, and starting and stopping with a few back stitches, slowly machine stitch a ¼″ seam allowance around the perimeter of the acorn. End the stitching near the top right star point to leave an approximate 1½″–2″ opening for turning the mug mat right side out. Remove the pins.

Leave opening for turning right sides out.

4. Carefully turn the mug mat right side out through the opening, using the eraser-end of a pencil or a turning tool to smooth out the stitched edges to achieve a nice shape. When you're pleased with the look of the acorn, use a hot iron to press the mug mat, turning the raw edges of the opening inward. Anchor the edges of the acorn with pins, ensuring the raw edges of the opening fall inside the pinned edge. Use your sewing machine to edgestitch the entire perimeter of the mug mat, three or four threads inside the edges.

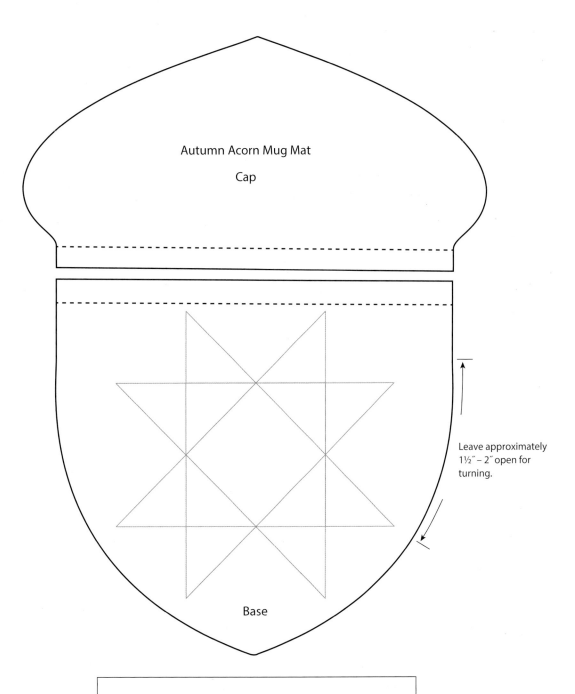

Autumn Acorn Mug Mat

Cap

Base

Leave approximately
1½″ – 2″ open for
turning.

Notes:

• A ¼″ seam allowance is built into the acorn shape
along the outer edges.

• When cutting the acorn pattern pieces, cut along the
outer edge of the shapes, exactly next to the lines.

Pocket Change

Save your loose pocket change, add it together, and what happens? Something that started out small can really add up! Save and gather bits of your favorite prints, cut them into triangles and squares, and like your pocket change, watch them add up into a mini that becomes so much more than the sum of its parts.

MATERIALS

Yardage is based on a 42″ width of useable fabric after prewashing and removing selvages.

+ 4 fat quarters (18″ × 21″) of assorted cream prints for blocks and sashing
+ 1 fat quarter of brown print for sashing, border, and binding
+ 24 chubby sixteenths (9″ × 10½″) of assorted prints for blocks, sashing, and border
+ 1 yard of fabric for backing
+ 32″ × 32″ square of batting

CUTTING

Cut all pieces across the width of the fabric in the order given unless otherwise noted.

From *each* of the 4 assorted cream prints, cut:
8 squares, 3″ × 3″ (combined total of 32); cut each square in half diagonally *once* to yield 2 triangles (combined total of 64)
Reserve the remainder of the 4 assorted cream prints.

From the remainder of the 4 assorted cream prints, cut a *combined* total of:
40 rectangles, 1½″ × 2½″
64 squares, 1½″ × 1½″

From *each* of 16 of the chubby sixteenths of assorted prints, cut:
2 squares, 3″ × 3″ (combined total of 32); cut each square in half diagonally *once* to yield 2 triangles (combined total of 64). Keep the triangles organized by print.
Reserve the remainder of the 16 assorted prints.

From the brown print for the binding, cut:
6 binding strips, 2½″ × 21″ (For my chubby binding method on page 126, reduce the strip width to 2″.)
Reserve the remainder of the brown print.

From the 8 unused prints, the remainder of the 16 used assorted prints, and the remainder of the brown print, cut a *combined* total of:
285 squares, 1½″ × 1½″ (For added versatility when stitching the patchwork, you may wish to cut a handful of extra squares.)

PIECING THE PINWHEEL VARIATION BLOCKS

Sew all pieces with right sides together using a ¼″ seam allowance unless otherwise noted. Press the seam allowances as indicated by the arrows or otherwise specified.

1. Select a set of four matching print triangles (referred to "dark" from this point forward), and four assorted cream triangles. Join a dark and a cream triangle along the long diagonal edges. Press. Repeat to piece a total of four units. Use a rotary cutter and a small acrylic ruler featuring a center diagonal line to trim each unit to a measurement of 2½″ square, removing the dog-ear points in the same step. Repeat to piece a total of 16 sets of half-square-triangle units, with each set featuring one matching dark print.

Make 16 sets of 4 units, 2½″ × 2½″.

2. Lay out one set of half-square-triangle units in two horizontal rows as shown to form a pinwheel. Join the pieces in each row. Press. Join the rows. Press. Repeat

to piece a total of 16 pinwheel units measuring 4½″ square, including the seam allowances.

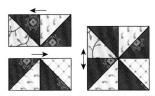

Make 16 pinwheel units, 4½″ × 4½″.

3. Use a pencil and an acrylic ruler to draw a diagonal sewing line from corner to corner on the wrong side of each cream 1½″ square. Layer a prepared square onto two opposite corners of a pieced pinwheel unit from step 2. Stitch the squares along the drawn diagonal lines. Fold the resulting inner triangles open, aligning the corners with the corners of the pinwheel unit. Trim away the excess layers beneath the top triangles, leaving ¼″ seam allowances. In the same manner, add cream triangles to the two remaining pinwheel corners. Repeat to complete a total of 16 Pinwheel Variation blocks measuring 4½″ square, including the seam allowances.

Make 16 Pinwheel Variation blocks, 4½″ × 4½″.

Pocket Change

Finished quilt size: 25½″ × 25½″ ◆ **Finished block size: 4″ × 4″**

Designed and pieced by Kim Diehl. Machine quilted by Connie Tabor.

PIECING THE QUILT CENTER

1. Choosing the prints randomly, join a dark 1½″ square to each end of a cream 1½″ × 2½″ rectangle. Press. Repeat to sew a total of 40 sashing units measuring 1½″ × 4½″, including the seam allowances.

Make 40 sashing units, 1½″ × 4½″.

2. Referring to the illustration, join four pieced sashing units and five assorted dark 1½″ squares to make a sashing row. Press. Repeat to piece a total of five sashing rows measuring 1½″ × 21½″, including the seam allowances.

Make 5 sashing rows, 1½″ × 21½″.

3. Lay out four Pinwheel Variation blocks and five pieced sashing units in alternating positions as shown. Join the pieces. Press. Repeat to piece a total of four block rows measuring 4½″ × 21½″, including the seam allowances.

Make 4 block rows, 4½″ × 21½″.

4. Lay out the four block rows and the five sashing rows in alternating positions as shown. Join the rows. Press. The pieced quilt center should measure 21½″ square, including the seam allowances.

Quilt center assembly

PIECING AND ADDING THE CHECKERBOARD BORDER

1. Using the remaining dark 1½″ squares, lay out 21 squares end to end. Join the squares. Press the seam allowances in one direction. Repeat to piece a total of four rows measuring 1½″ × 21½″, including the seam allowances.

2. Join two rows, with one row rotated to enable the seams to nest together, to make a checkerboard border strip. Press the seam allowances open. Repeat to piece a total of two checkerboard strips measuring 2½″ × 21½″, including the seam allowances. Referring to the quilt pictured on page 107, join these rows to the right and left sides of the quilt top. Press the seam allowances toward the border strips.

3. Using 25 squares for each row, repeat step 1 to piece and press four patchwork rows measuring 1½″ × 25½″, including the seam allowances. Referring to step 2, join and press the 25½″-long patchwork rows to make two checkerboard units. Join these units to the top and bottom edges of the quilt top. Press the seam allowances toward the border strips.

◆ **EXTRA SNIPPET** ◆

"Planned" Scrappy Patchwork

When stitching my scrappy projects, I find that the first handful of units come together easily when I have plenty of prints to choose from, but as I approach the end of my stitching it can be more challenging to arrange the prints in a pleasing way when there are fewer choices. To compensate for this, I've learned to pause when I'm about three-quarters through my piecing, evaluate the prints that remain, and lay them out in pairs as I intend to join them to ensure there will be a good balance of color. Taking a moment for a bit of pre-planning means that I'll be just as happy with the last unit as I was with my first one, and the patchwork will sparkle!

COMPLETING THE QUILT

Layer and baste the quilt top, batting, and backing. Quilt the layers. The featured quilt is free-motion machine quilted in a design of repeating curved curls. Join the brown binding strips to make one length and use it to bind the quilt.

Sunshine and Shadow

Lavish leaves in bright and shadowed hues bring the feel of an old-fashioned cottage garden—no weeding or watering required! This little quilt is perfect for incorporating the smallest saved scraps, giving them a second chance to shine. Even "wallflower" prints that are a bit different can add bits of sparkle—simply use them more than once for a balanced and intentional look.

MATERIALS

Yardages are based on a 42″ width of useable fabric after prewashing and removing selvages.

- 4 fat eighths of assorted cream prints for patchwork and appliqués
- 24 chubby sixteenths (9″ × 10½″) of assorted prints for patchwork, appliqués, and binding
- 1 fat eighth of cranberry print for border
- ⅝ yard of fabric for backing
- 21″ × 21″ square of batting
- Freezer paper
- Water-soluble and acid-free glue for fabric, in liquid and stick form
- Supplies for your favorite appliqué method
- Liquid seam sealant, such as Fray Check, is optional but suggested

CUTTING

Cut all pieces across the width of the fabric in the order given unless otherwise noted. For greater ease, cutting for the appliqués is provided separately.

From the assorted cream prints, cut a *combined* total of:
18 squares, 3″ × 3″; cut each square in half diagonally *once* to yield 2 triangles (combined total of 36)
36 rectangles, 1¼″ × 3¼″

From the 24 assorted prints (collectively referred to as "darks," cut a *combined* total of:
18 squares, 3″ × 3″; cut each square in half diagonally *once* to yield 2 triangles (combined total of 36)
36 rectangles, 1¼″ × 3¼″
Enough 2½″-wide strips in random lengths to make a 68″ length of binding when joined together end to end. (For my chubby binding method on page 126, reduce the strip width to 2″.)

From the cranberry print, cut:
2 strips, 1½″ × 12½″
2 strips, 1½″ × 14½″

PIECING THE HALF-SQUARE-TRIANGLE BLOCKS

Sew all pieces with right sides together using a ¼″ seam allowance unless otherwise noted. Press the seam allowances as indicated by the arrows or otherwise specified.

Join a cream and a dark triangle along the long diagonal edges. Press. Use a rotary cutter and an acrylic ruler to trim the unit to measure 2½″ square, removing the dog-ear points in the same step. Repeat to piece a total of 36 Half-Square-Triangle blocks.

Make 36 units, 2½″ × 2½″.

PIECING THE QUILT CENTER

Please note that the appliqués will be cut and stitched once the quilt top has been completed.

1. Lay out the Half-Square-Triangle blocks in six horizontal rows of six blocks, positioning the blocks as shown to form the quilt design. Join the blocks in each row. Press the seam allowances of each row in an alternating direction, so the seams will nest together when the rows are joined. Join the rows. Press. The pieced quilt center should measure 12½" square, including the seam allowances.

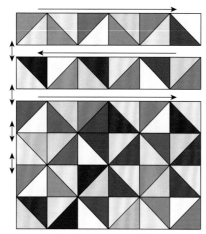

Quilt center assembly

2. Join a cranberry 1½" × 12½" strip to the right and left sides of the quilt center. Press. Join the cranberry 1½" × 14½" strips to the top and bottom of the quilt center. Press. The pieced quilt top should measure 14½" square, including the seam allowances.

3. This step is optional, but I suggest applying a thin line of liquid seam sealant around the perimeter of the quilt top to preserve the seam allowances during the appliqué steps.

APPLIQUÉING THE QUILT CENTER

1. Join a cream and a dark 1¼" × 3¼" rectangle along the long edges. Press. Repeat to piece a total of 36 pieced rectangles measuring 2" × 3¼", including the seam allowances.

Make pieced rectangles, 2" × 3¼".

2. Referring to "Invisible Machine Appliqué" and "Preparing Freezer-Paper Pattern Pieces" beginning on page 121, prepare 36 appliqué pattern pieces using the leaf pattern below.

3. Using the freezer-paper pattern pieces and pieced rectangles from step 1, cut and prepare the appliqués as described in "Preparing Appliqués from Fabric" on page 122. Be sure to align the dashed line of the pattern with the seamline of the rectangles.

4. Position an appliqué onto each Half-Square-Triangle block with the cream half on the dark triangle. Center and baste the appliqués as instructed in "Basting Appliqués" on page 123. Follow the steps provided in "Stitching the Appliqués" on page 124 to stitch the appliqués in place, or use your own favorite method, removing the freezer paper pattern pieces when done.

Position and stitch an appliqué to each block.

COMPLETING THE QUILT

Layer and baste the quilt top, batting, and backing. Quilt the layers. The featured quilt is machine quilted outlining each appliqué to emphasize its shape. A line of small-scale feathers is stitched onto the cranberry border, with the direction of the feathers radiating out from the center position toward each corner. Join the 2½"-wide random-length strips to make one length of binding, and use it to bind the quilt.

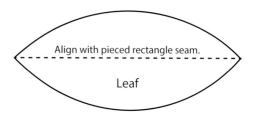

Align with pieced rectangle seam.

Leaf

Pattern does not include seam allowances.

FINISHED QUILT SIZE: 14½″ × 14½″ ◆ **FINISHED BLOCK SIZE:** 2″ × 2″
Designed and pieced by Kim Diehl. Machine quilted by Deborah Poole.

Wash Day

This charming little mini is equal parts skill-building as you ace the points on your center star, and casual kicked-back sewing as you stitch the simple rail fence units. Surround your scrappy quilt center with bold and chunky half-square-triangles, and you've got yourself a quick-to-sew quilt that will stand the test of time.

MATERIALS

Yardages are based on a 42″ width of useable fabric after prewashing and removing selvages.

+ 1 fat quarter (18″ × 21″) of black print for patchwork and binding
+ Approximately ½ yard worth of assorted-print scraps for patchwork
+ Approximately ½ yard worth of assorted cream scraps for patchwork
+ 1 fat quarter of print for backing
+ 18″ × 21″ rectangle of batting

CUTTING

Cut all pieces across the width of the fabric in the order given unless otherwise noted.

From the fat quarter of black print, cut:
4 binding strips, 2½″ × 21″ (for my chubby binding method provided on page 126, reduce the strip width to 2″)
Reserve the remainder of the black print.

From the assorted-print scraps, and the remainder of the black print (collectively referred to as "dark"), cut a *combined* total of:
8 squares, 1½″ × 1½″
1 square, 2½″ × 2½″, for the star center square (I cut this piece from the reserved black print)
64 rectangles, 1¼″ × 2½″
12 squares, 3″ × 3″; cut each square in half diagonally *once* to yield 2 triangles (combined total of 24)
    Note: For a scrappier look, I cut 24 squares to yield 2 triangles each, and used just 1 triangle from each print—the choice is yours!
4 squares, 2½″ × 2½″, for the border corner squares

From the assorted cream scraps, cut a *combined* total of:
32 rectangles, 1″ × 2½″
4 rectangles, 1½″ × 2½″
4 squares, 1½″ × 1½″
12 squares, 3″ × 3″; cut each square in half diagonally *once* to yield 2 triangles (combined total of 24)

PIECING THE QUILT-CENTER UNITS

Sew all pieces with right sides together using a ¼″ seam allowance unless otherwise noted. Press the seam allowances as indicated by the arrows or otherwise specified.

1. Use a pencil and an acrylic ruler to draw a diagonal sewing line from corner to corner on the wrong side of the eight dark 1½″ squares. Layer a prepared square onto one end of a cream 1½″ × 2½″ rectangle. Stitch the pair together along the drawn line. Fold the resulting inner triangle open, aligning the corner with the corner of the cream rectangle. Press. Trim away the layers beneath the top triangle, leaving a ¼″ seam allowance. In the same manner, add a mirror-image star point to the remaining end of the rectangle. Repeat to piece a total of four flying-geese units measuring 1½″ × 2½″, including the seam allowances.

Make 4 units, 1½″ × 2½″.

2. Lay out the four flying-geese units, the 2½″ square cut for the star center, and the four cream 1½″ squares in three horizontal rows as shown. Join the pieces in each row. Press. Join the rows. Press. The pieced star should measure 4½″ square, including the seam allowances.

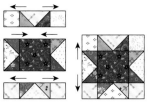

Make 1 star unit, 4½″ × 4½″.

3. Join a dark 1¼″ × 2½″ rectangle to each long side of a cream 1″ × 2½″ rectangle using a slightly scant ¼″ seam allowance. Press. Use a rotary cutter and an acrylic ruler to square up the slightly oversized rail fence unit to measure 2½″ square, including the seam allowances. Repeat to piece a total of 32 rail fence units.

Make 32 rail fence units, 2½″ × 2½″.

Wash Day

Finished quilt size: 16½″ × 16½″

Designed and pieced by Kim Diehl. Machine quilted by Rebecca Silbaugh.

PIECING THE QUILT CENTER

1. Referring to the illustration, lay out four rail fence units in two horizontal rows. Join the units in each row. Press. Repeat to piece a total of eight Quadruple Rail Fence blocks measuring 4½" square, including the seam allowances.

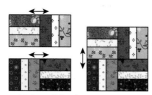

Make 8 blocks, 4½" × 4½".

2. Join three Quadruple Rail Fence blocks end to end. Press. Repeat to piece a total of two rail fence rows measuring 4½" × 12½", including the seam allowances.

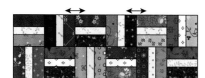

Make 2 Fail Fence rows, 4½" × 12½".

3. Join the two remaining Quadruple Rail Fence blocks from step 1 to the right and left sides of the star unit. Press. The pieced center star row should measure 4½" × 12½", including the seam allowances.

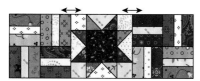

Make 1 center star row, 4½" × 12½".

4. Join a rail fence row from step 2 to each long side of the center star row. Press the seam allowances away from the center row. The pieced quilt center should measure 12½" square, including the seam allowances.

PIECING AND ADDING THE BORDER

1. Join a dark and a cream print 3" triangle along the long diagonal edges. Press. Use a rotary cutter and an acrylic ruler to trim the unit to 2½" square, removing the dog-ear points in the same step. Repeat to piece a total of 24 half-square-triangle units.

Make 24 units, 2½" × 2½".

2. Join six half-square units end to end as shown to make a triangle row. Press. Repeat to piece a total of two triangle rows and two mirror-image triangle rows measuring 2½" × 12½", including the seam allowances.

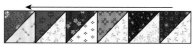

Make 2 border rows, 2½" × 12½".

Make 2 mirror-image border rows, 2½" × 12½".

3. Referring to the quilt pictured on page 117, join the mirror-image triangle rows to the right and left sides of the quilt center. Press the seam allowances toward the quilt center. Join the four dark 2½" squares cut for the border to the ends of the remaining two triangle rows. Press the seam allowances toward the squares. Join these pieced rows to the top and bottom of the quilt center. Press the seam allowances toward the center of the quilt.

COMPLETING THE QUILT

Layer and baste the quilt top, batting, and backing. Quilt the layers. The featured quilt is machine quilted with straight diagonal lines from point to point on the star unit, with straight lines echoing the star shape in the cream background areas. Half-circles are stitched radiating out from each dark straight side of the rail fence units, and straight lines echoing the triangle angles in the border. Join the black binding strips to make one length and use it to bind the quilt.

Kim's Quiltmaking Basics

You'll find the basic information needed to make the quilts in this book in the section that follows, with the information and techniques provided in simple, approachable steps.

Cutting from the Width of the Fabric

Patchwork pieces are typically cut from the width of the fabric, meaning that you cut from selvage to selvage. Cutting from smaller precuts such as chubby sixteenths, charm squares, etc., can make it more difficult to determine the width of the fabric because the selvages may be missing. An easy way to tell the width of fabric direction from any piece of cloth is to hold two opposite edges and gently pull them apart. If there's a bit of stretch when pulled, you've found the width of the fabric. If there is no give to the cloth when pulled, rotate the piece of cloth and try this step again from the alternate direction. The direction with the most stretch will be the width of fabric, and you can now position the piece of cloth accordingly to make your cuts.

Cutting Multiple Prints for Scrappy Quilts

When a project calls for numerous prints to be cut, I've learned that I'll get the best and quickest results when I layer and prepare them on my pressing surface first. Here are the steps I use:

1. Choose up to six prints for the group to be cut, layering the first print onto the pressing surface.

Give the cloth a light misting of Best Press (a starch alternative) or water and press it smooth and flat with a hot iron.

2. Continue layering, misting, and pressing each new print, roughly aligning the edges along one side and the bottom with the previously positioned print, to form a stack. This layering and pressing approach will help meld the fabric layers together for easier cutting with minimal shifting, and the misting step will give the fabric added body for a crisp texture for great piecing results.

Note: If your mix of prints includes a stripe or a pronounced pattern, save and position it as the top layer of the stack. Adding these types of prints as the topmost layer will enable you to position the press stack well for cutting, producing cut patchwork pieces with lines that run straight and true.

3. Transfer the pressed stack to the cutting board, aligning the topmost print with the cutting grid to ensure the weave of the cloth and the direction of the print is positioned well, and make the specified cuts.

Pinning

I suggest pinning your patchwork at regular intervals, including all sewn seams. My best tip for pinning, which helps me achieve great results when piecing my own quilts, is to "pin weave" the last pin at the tail end of each patchwork unit, where the cloth receives the most stress from handling. Pin weaving simply means to weave the point of the pin through the cloth *twice* as shown in the illustration, which will keep in securely in place and prevent it from wiggling free.

Another benefit of pin weaving is that you can lay your fingertip over this last woven pin and use it to guide the tail end of the patchwork slowly under the presser foot—you'll eliminate fishtailing and produce a consistent seam allowance from start to finish.

MACHINE PIECING

Unless specified otherwise, always join your patchwork with right sides together using a ¼″ seam allowance. I suggest using neutral-colored thread in both the needle and bobbin, rather than white, because your stitches will blend better with a variety of prints and be less visible when the seams are pressed open.

Last, I recommend shortening your machine's stitch length slightly because this will produce secure seams from edge to edge, with stitches that nestle into the fabric for more invisible seam lines. For my sewing machine, I reduce the length from a standard setting of 2.2 down to 1.8.

PRESSING PATCHWORK

I'm often asked how I press my patchwork because the blocks lay beautifully flat and smooth when finished. Here are the steps I use:

1. Place the pieced unit on the pressing surface with the fabric you want to press *toward* positioned on top. Briefly touch your hot iron to the top layer of cloth to warm it, and fold it back to expose the seam. Run your fingernail along the line of thread to open the cloth all the way to the seam, and finish pressing from the front of the unit.

Press open.

2. Once the block has been completed, this is the step that really produces the magic. Lay the block *wrong* side up on the pressing surface and give it a light misting of Best Press (or water). Methodically work your way across the block to press the seams from the *back* to ensure they're laying smooth, flat, and in the intended direction. This approach sets the seams nicely in place and eliminates the sheen that can sometimes form on the front of the fabric from the iron.

KIM'S INVISIBLE MACHINE APPLIQUÉ TECHNIQUE

For this appliqué method, you'll need the following items in addition to your standard sewing and quiltmaking supplies:

* .004 monofilament (invisible thread) in smoke and clear colors

* Awl or stiletto with a sharp point

* Embroidery scissors with a sharp point

* Freezer paper

* Iron with a pronounced point for pressing shapes and with a nonstick surface, if possible

* Fabric glue in liquid and stick form water-soluble and acid-free (my favorite liquid brand is Quilter's Choice Basting Glue by Beacon Adhesives)

* Open-toe presser foot, or a foot with a clear acrylic center insert

* Pressing board with a firm surface (wool pressing mats work beautifully)

* Sewing machine with adjustable tension control, able to produce a zigzag stitch in a tiny size (see page 124 for an example)

* Size 75/11 (or smaller) machine-quilting needles

* Tweezers with a rounded tip

Preparing Pattern Tracing Templates

When making a tracing *template*, only one will be needed for any given shape, because it's simply a tool used to trace and cut the individual freezer-paper pattern *pieces* used to prepare the fabric appliqués for stitching. Here are the template preparation steps I use:

1. Cut a single piece of freezer paper, about twice as big as your shape. Lay the paper over the pattern sheet, waxy side down, and trace the shape onto one end of the paper.

2. Fold the traced paper in half, waxy sides together, and use a hot, dry iron to fuse the layers together.

3. Cut out the template exactly along the drawn line (the seam allowance will be added later).

Preparing Freezer-Paper Pattern Pieces

Pattern *pieces* are the individual paper shapes that will be used to prepare the fabric appliqués for stitching after the pattern *template* has been used to trace them. Here are the steps I use:

1. Use the pattern template (when many appliqués are needed) or trace directly from the pattern sheet (if only a small handful of appliqués are needed) to transfer the shape onto one end of a strip of freezer paper, in a width that will accommodate the appliqué size.

2. Accordion fold the strip up to six layers deep (more than six layers will feel bulky and be difficult to cut). For curvy or more complex shapes, you may wish to limit the layers to four, to achieve better control when cutting.

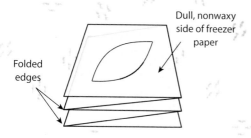

Folded edges

Dull, nonwaxy side of freezer paper

3. Anchor the center of the shape with a straight pin or staple the paper in the background areas around the shape to stabilize the layers and prevent shifting. Cut out the shape exactly along the drawn line to produce up to six pattern pieces with each cut.

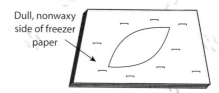

Dull, nonwaxy side of freezer paper

4. Repeat steps 1–3 to make the number of pieces needed. Keep in mind that when using the accordion-fold method for shapes that aren't perfectly symmetrical will produce mirror-image shapes from every other piece of freezer paper when the layers are separated. To make multiple identical pieces from non-symmetrical shapes, stack individual freezer-paper layers together instead of using an accordion-folded strip, all with the waxy side down.

Preparing Appliqués from Fabric

1. Apply a small dab of fabric glue stick to the center of the dull, nonwaxy side of the freezer-paper pattern piece and position it onto the wrong side of the fabric, waxy side *up*. When preparing more than one appliqué from a single piece of fabric, leave approximately ½" between each shape.

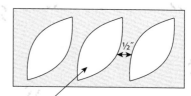

½"

Wrong side of fabric, freezer paper waxy side up

2. Use embroidery scissors to cut out each shape, adding an approximately ¼" seam allowance. If this technique is new to you, applying a piece of quarter-inch quilter's tape to your thumbnail on the hand that will be holding the appliqué as you cut the shape, will give you a great visual for adding the right amount of seam allowance. Adding more than a ¼" seam allowance will result in extra bulk and make it difficult to turn under and press in later steps.

Pressing Appliqué Seam Allowances

For the following steps, keep in mind that if you're right-handed you'll work from right to left as you prepare the shapes; if you're left-handed, reverse the direction and work from left to right.

1. Set your iron to the "cotton" setting, with no steam (steam will fuse the fabric more firmly to the freezer-paper pattern, making it difficult to remove, and you'll burn your fingers!). Beginning at a straight edge or a gentle curve, *not* at a corner or point, use your fingertip to smooth the fabric onto the back of the appliqué so it's resting on the waxy surface of the pattern piece. As you slide your finger from the fabric toward the center of the shape away from the appliqué edge, immediately follow behind with the tip of your iron to fuse the fabric to the waxy surface of the pattern piece. Let the iron rest in place as you repeat to draw the next bit of seam-allowance fabric onto the pattern piece, as this will provide extra heat and help the fabric firmly fuse to the paper.

Direct seam allowance toward center of shape.

2. As you approach the corner of the shape, fold the fabric seam allowance toward the back of the piece so it extends beyond the pattern point as shown, keeping the fabric snugged up against the paper edge. Press this first fold at the corner of the shape. Fold over the seam allowance on the remaining side of the point and continue pressing to complete the piece.

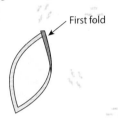

First fold

3. Apply a small dab of fabric glue stick under the flap of the fabric seam allowance fold at each point. Use the tip of a sharp awl to grab and drag the fabric in and away from the appliqué edge so it will be hidden from the front. Use the point of the iron to fuse the seam allowance in place, removing the awl as the fabric is pressed.

Basting Appliqués

After laying out your appliqué design to ensure the pieces fit well and are positioned to your liking, you have the option of pinning them, thread basting them, *or* glue basting, which is my preferred method. Glue basting keeps the shapes securely anchored in place, prevents shifting, and eliminates the shrinkage that can sometimes occur to the background of the block as the appliqués are stitched. Here are the glue-basting steps I use:

1. Choose an appliqué positioned in your layout. Without removing the shape from where it's resting on the background, fold back one half of the appliqué to expose the back, making the pressed seam allowance visible. Apply small dots of liquid fabric glue at approximately ¼" to ½" intervals along the pressed fabric seam allowance around the exposed back portion of the appliqué, making sure to place a dot of glue on any points. Reposition the glue-basted portion of the appliqué onto the background, pressing it firmly in place with your hand. Repeat with the remainder of the shape.

2. Once all of the shapes have been glue basted, use a hot, dry iron from the back of the block to heat set the glue dots and firmly anchor the appliqués to the fabric.

Preparing Your Sewing Machine

1. Insert a size 75/11 or smaller needle into the sewing machine and thread it with monofilament thread; the smoke color works well for medium and dark prints, and clear is generally the best choice for lighter, brighter prints.

2. Wind the bobbin with neutral-colored all-purpose thread in a sturdy, *not fine*, weight. (Heavier weight thread will resist pulling up through the fabric to the surface of the appliqué for invisible stitches, while fine thread can tend to slide through the layers to the surface more easily, making your stitches visible.) I also suggest avoiding prewound bobbins, as they can make it difficult to regulate the thread tension of your sewing machine to achieve secure, invisible results.

Note: If your sewing machine's bobbin case features a "finger" with a special eye for use with embroidery techniques, threading your bobbin thread through this opening will help further regulate the tension and produce ideal stitches.

3. Set the sewing machine to the zigzag stitch and adjust the width and length settings to achieve a tiny stitch as shown below. Next, reduce the tension setting (a level of 1 or 2 for most machines) until the stitches on a test piece and sturdy and secure, with the bobbin thread remaining underneath the top layer of the block and no visible dots appearing.

〰〰〰〰〰〰〰〰〰〰〰〰〰〰〰

Approximate stitch size

STITCHING THE APPLIQUÉS

When time permits, I love hand stitching my appliqués, and at this point of the project you can still make this choice using a needle and matching thread in a fine weight. Once stitched, refer to "Removing Paper Pattern Pieces" on page 125 to complete the piece.

For projects where my goal is to finish quickly, machine stitching the appliqués is my go-to choice because it produces invisibly stitched, sturdy appliqués in a fraction of the time needed for hand stitching. Here are the steps I use:

1. Slide the basted block under the presser foot from front to back to direct the threads to the back of the machine, with the needle poised above the appliqué you'll be stitching. With the appliqué positioned to the left of the needle at a straight or gently curved edge, *not* a corner or point, drop the needle down into the appliqué a few threads in from the edge. Grab the threads from the needle and bobbin behind the presser foot, or lay your fingertip securely over them to prevent them from pulling up into the sewing machine, and begin stitching.

2. Take two or three stitches, release the threads, and then begin stitching the perimeter of the appliqué; stop and clip the top thread after about an inch of the appliqué has been sewn. As you continue working around the appliqué, train your eyes to watch the outer stitches, ensuring they drop into the background exactly next to the appliqué, and the inner stitches will automatically fall inside the shape where they should.

3. As you approach the point of the appliqué, stitch to the position where the outer stitch lands exactly next to the point and drops into the background, and stop. Pivot the block and continue stitching along the remainder of the shape, overlapping your starting point by approximately ¼". If your machine offers a locking-stitch feature, use it and clip the thread. If your machine doesn't offer this option, extend the length of your overlapped stitches to about ½″ from your starting point. (The greatest benefit of using a locking stitch is that it resets the sewing machine and brings the needle back to the starting position, making it easy to align each new appliqué under the needle.)

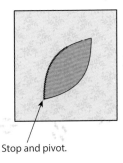

Stop and pivot.

4. For designs with two or more appliqués spaced closely together, I recommend taking the "string appliqué" approach. This means that as the stitching for each appliqué is finished, instead of clipping the threads, lift the presser foot and slide the block background to the next appliqué without moving it from the sewing machine surface. Continue stitching in this manner to complete the design, and then carefully clip the threads between the appliqués.

Removing Paper Pattern Pieces

1. From the wrong side of the block, use embroidery scissors to carefully pinch and cut through the fabric underneath the appliqué approximately ¼″ in from the stitch edge. Trim away the background fabric underneath the appliqué, leaving a generous ¼″ seam allowance inside the shape to keep it secure.

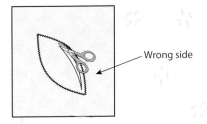

Wrong side

2. To remove the pattern piece, grasp the appliqué edge between the thumb and finger of one hand, and grab the seam allowance immediately opposite with the other hand. Give a gentle but firm tug to free the paper edge from the line of stitching. Slide your fingertip between the paper and the appliqué to loosen the pattern piece where it's been anchored with glue stick, and pull the paper straight out from the stitch seam as you work around the shape. Use tweezers with a rounded tip to remove any paper piece that might be stuck in a point or in an area of the seam. If the paper is too small to easily grab and remove, it's too small to worry about!

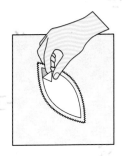

3. After all paper pattern pieces have been removed, lay the block wrong side up on the pressing surface and *briefly* press the fabric seam allowances with a hot iron to ensure they're lying smooth and flat.

QUILTING THE QUILT

There are lots of options available for finishing your quilt.

If you choose to have your quilt top machine quilted, you'll want to be sure the seams have been pressed well and are lying flat and in the intended direction. Stay-stitching the patchwork around the perimeter of the top, about ⅛″ in from the raw edge, is also a good idea because it will keep the seams from pulling apart as it's being handled.

Last, I suggest applying a thin line of liquid seam sealant along the perimeter of the quilt top to prevent the fabric from fraying and keep the ¼″ seam allowance intact.

CHUBBY BINDING

Complete step-by-step instructions for traditional binding can be found on the C&T website as previously referenced. My more unconventional "chubby binding" features a single layer of binding that has a traditional look from the front, and a wide width of binding on the back to beautifully frame your quilt backing and reduce bult at the mitered corners. Here are the steps I use:

1. Cut the binding strips 2″ wide (instead of the traditional 2½″ width) in the length instructed in the project directions. Join the strips end to end using straight, *not* diagonal, seams.

2. Using a bias-tape maker designed to produce 1″-wide double-fold tape, feed the binding strip through the tool *wrong side up* so the resulting folds of the strip are visible as you work. As the strip emerges from the maker, press it flat with a hot iron so the raw folded edges meet at the center of the strip; this pressing step will automatically direct the seam allowances where the strip has been joined to one side, resting flat and in the same direction.

3. Open the pressed binding strip along the top edge only, turn the end under approximately ½″ to hide the raw edge, and position it onto the quilt top at one side, not a corner. Pin and then stitch the binding in place along the first side of the quilt, stopping ¼″ from the first corner, and take a few backstitches (or use a locking stitch).

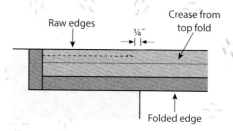

Raw edges   Crease from top fold   ¼″   Folded edge

4. Make a fold in the binding, bringing it back down onto itself to square the corner, and then pin the remainder in place along the next side of the quilt. Rotate and position the corner of the quilt under the presser foot and stitch the next section of pinned binding. Continue in this manner to sew the binding to the entire quilt top, cutting the raw end about 1″ beyond your starting point.

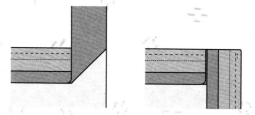

5. Bring the wide folded edge of the binding from the front of the quilt to the back, mitering the corners, and pin it in place. From the back of the quilt, use a needle and matching thread to hand sew a blind stitch along the binding edge and anchor it in place.

◆ EXTRA SNIPPET ◆

Tidy Binding Creases

Depending upon the thickness of the batting used in the quilt, the top binding crease may not fall exactly at the edge of the quilt. If this occurs, simply give the finished binding a light press from the front of the quilt with a hot iron to smooth it out.

About the Author

Kim became a quilter almost by accident when she chanced upon a sampler quilt pattern at a sidewalk sale in the late 1990s, fell in love with the design, and impulsively decided to try something she knew nothing about. Without a mentor or any quilting experience, she bought everything needed and worked her way through the steps one by one. By the time her quilt was finished, Kim was hooked!

Soon after completing her first quilt, Kim learned of a national quilting contest hosted by *American Patchwork & Quilting* magazine. Not realizing how little she knew about her new hobby, Kim entered the contest, and with just the third quilt she'd ever made, won! This win gave her the opportunity to submit several designs to the magazine for consideration, and to her surprise, each design was accepted. With her fourth quilt Kim began publishing, and in the years since, more than 25 of her original designs have appeared on the pages of *American Patchwork & Quilting* magazine. Magazines led to books, and Kim has been very blessed to author more than twenty quilting titles, most in her popular "Simple" series.

When given the chance to try her hand at fabric design for Henry Glass Fabrics, Kim jumped at this opportunity, trusting her instincts and sense of color to guide her. To date, she has more than 50 quilting collections under her belt, and still counting!

Kim spends her time close to home these days gardening and baking, enjoying time with her husband and two grandies, volunteering at school, and taking care of her pack of pooches that includes two rescue dogs. Life is good!

Instagram: @kim_diehl_quilts

CREATIVE SPARK
ONLINE LEARNING

Crafty courses to become an expert maker...

From their studio to yours, Creative Spark instructors are teaching you how to create and become a master of your craft. So not only do you get a look inside their creative space, you also get to be a part of engaging courses that would typically be a one or multi-day workshop from the comfort of your home.

Creative Spark is not your one-size-fits-all online learning experience. We welcome you to be who you are, share, create, and belong.

Scan for a gift from us!